Helion & Company Limited
Unit 8 Amherst Business Centre
Budbrooke Road
Warwick
CV34 5WE
England
Tel. 01926 499 619
Email: info@helion.co.uk
Website: www.helion.co.uk
Twitter: @helionbooks
Visit our blog https://helionbooks.wordpress.com/

Text © Richard A. Rinaldi 2024
Photographs © as individually credited
Colour profiles: by David Bocquelet, Renato Dalmaso and Rolando Ungolini © Helion & Company 2024
Diagrams: Tom Cooper © Helion & Company 2024

Typeset by Oliver Barstow, Milan, Italy
Cover design by Paul Hewitt, Battlefield Design (www.battlefield-design.co.uk)

Every reasonable effort has been made to trace copyright holders and to obtain their permission for the use of copyright material. The author and publisher apologise for any errors or omissions in this work, and would be grateful if notified of any corrections that should be incorporated in future reprints or editions of this book.

ISBN 978-1-804515-85-3

British Library Cataloguing-in-Publication Data
A catalogue record for this book is available from the British Library

All rights reserved. No part of this publication may be reproduced, stored in a retrieval system, or transmitted, in any form, or by any means, electronic, mechanical, photocopying, recording or otherwise, without the express written consent of Helion & Company Limited.

We always welcome receiving book proposals from prospective authors.

I0886420

CONTENTS

Note: In order to simplify the use of this book, all names, locations and geographic designations are as provided in *The Times World Atlas*, or other traditionally accepted major sources of reference, as of the time of described events.

ABBREVIATIONS AND ACRONYMS

APC	Armoured Personnel Carrier
AR	Army Reserve (Territorial Army to 2012)
ARRC	Allied Rapid Reaction Corps; NATO corps HQ commanded by a British lieutenant general
ATC	Army Training Centre
ATk	Anti-tank
ATR	Army Training Regiment
CBRN	chemical, biological, radiological and nuclear (formerly NBC; nuclear, biological and chemical)
C-CBRN	counter-CBRN
CDS	Chief of the Defence Staff
CEMA	Cyber and Electro Magnetic Activities (new entity under *Future Soldier*)
CFA	Commander Field Army
CGS	Chief of the General Staff
CS	close support
CSM	Company Sergeant Major
CVR(T)	Combat Vehicle Reconnaissance (Tracked) (family of vehicles for recce and other duties)
ECM	electronic counter measures
EOD	explosive ordnance disposal
EW	electronic warfare
FTC	Force Troops Command; controlled most field units outside of infantry and armour; reorganised in 2019 as 6th (UK) Division and many assigned brigades reorganised or transferred
FV	Fighting Vehicle (used in some designations, e.g., FV432)
GMLRS	Guided Multi-Launch Rocket System (GPS-assisted 227mm rockets)
GOC	General Officer Commanding
GPMG	general purpose machine gun (7.62mm)
HMG	heavy machine gun (12.7mm; US .50-calibre)
HQ	Headquarters
HVM	High Velocity Missile (surface to air); SP version is on a Stormer vehicle
IED	improvised explosive device
Infra	infrastructure
ISR	intelligence, surveillance and reconnaissance
ISTAR	intelligence, surveillance, target acquisition and reconnaissance
JFC	Joint Forces Command; renamed Strategic Command in 2019
JHC	Joint Helicopter Command
LCT	landing craft tank
LCU	landing craft utility
LCVP	landing craft vehicles and personnel
LML	Lightweight Multiple Launcher; non-SP version of HVM SAM
LRG	Littoral Response Group; RM and RN task group
MBT	Main Battle Tank
MOD	Ministry of Defence
OCU	Operational Conversion Unit; teaches pilots how to fly a particular aircraft and the best tactics to take advantage of its performance
OPFOR	Opposition Force; unit specialising in serving as the enemy in field exercises
PJHQ	Permanent Joint Headquarters; plans for and controls all overseas operations of the British military
RHQ	Regimental HQ
RPOC	Regional Points of Command; they provide administrative support for all units (Regular, AR and cadet) within their territorial area
RSM	Regimental Sergeant Major
RSME	Royal School of Miliary Engineering
SAM	surface to air missile
SDSR	Strategic Defence and Security Review; 2010 plan to restructure UK armed forces; superseded by *Army 2020* for the Army
SFA	Security Force Assistance (to foreign armies)
SP	Self-propelled (artillery)
STA	surveillance and target acquisition
STRE	Specialist Team RE (small group with skills to support infrastructure and other projects)
TA	Territorial Army; renamed Army Reserve (AR) in 2012
UAS/V	Unmanned Aerial System/Vehicle (more commonly, drones; some are referred to as miniature [MUAS] or tactical [TUAS])
UKSF	UK Special Forces

AN EDITORIAL NOTE

All of the photographic images contained within this work are from the UK Ministry of Defence's Defence Imagery website (https://www.defenceimagery.mod.uk/) and have been reproduced under the terms of the Open Government Licence that can be found here: https://www.nationalarchives.gov.uk/doc/open-government-licence/version/3/

The reference given after each caption is the original filename given by the MoD on the Defence Imagery website. The captions used have been written by the author and/or Helion's editorial team, and in particular, the date and location given are based upon information contained in the official captions; other details may vary from the official caption.

One restriction of the terms of the Open Government Licence is that we are unable to reproduce images that show the faces of clearly identifiable individuals and this has sometimes restricted the choice of images that we have been to share with you in this work. Likewise, images of some of the newer items of equipment available under the terms of this licence are limited, particularly AFVs such as the Challenger 3. Nevertheless, we would like to take this opportunity to thank the UK Ministry of Defence for making so many very high-quality images available, without which it would have been impossible to comprehensively support the author's text with suitable photographs.

Every effort has been made by the author and the editorial team to ensure that this document is as current as possible at the time it goes to print. The election of a new government in the UK in the summer of 2024 means that here will inevitably be a new defence review and at the time of writing a new budget speech by the Chancellor of the Exchequer is imminent. In addition to which there are regular announcements of donations of equipment to Ukraine that may result in active types being unexpectedly retired or stockholdings reduced. Nevertheless, this work provides an important overview of the organisational development of the British Army, and by extension associated elements of the Royal Navy, Royal Marines and Royal Air Force, as experienced through the 2010s, into the 2020s, and beyond.

Helion Editorial Team, October 2024

ACKNOWLEDGEMENTS

As indicated elsewhere, I am grateful to my long-time trans-Atlantic pen pal and occasional collaborator, Graham Watson. Graham's sharing of information, documents, contacts and advice over the years have greatly improved my knowledge and understanding of the British Army.

I am especially grateful to Andy Miles, my editor at Helion. He worked diligently at turning my original manuscript into these books. Andy was judicious in suggesting changes and occasionally provided information that I had not yet uncovered. He commissioned the drawings and provided the detailed captions for them, along with selecting the many photographs that enhance the work. I am, of course, also grateful to other employees of Helion who have contributed to this publication.

Writing on the British military at this time is something of a moving target, with ongoing changes announced as the government assesses both the threats facing the country and the budgetary impact of defence spending. Even information and language posted to the Army, Royal Navy and Royal Air Force web sites changed (sometimes retroactively) while Volume 1 was being prepared for publication, which increased the burden on Andy as we tried to keep the book current while still going forward. In the end, however, any errors that might still occur are my responsibility.

Richard A. Rinaldi, October 2024

What is the British Army For?

Being combat ready for operations is our highest priority. The British Army is *ever vigilant, always ready and steadfast* in its commitment to the defence of the UK and its citizens.

The Army on One Page
British Army web site

INTRODUCTION

This work began around 2015 as a personal effort to show the organisation and locations of the British Army as it implemented the *Army 2020* restructuring. A large amount of detailed information was published by the Army on this topic. However, over time it became clear that the Army began making serious changes from the original plans, and this without the publicity accompanying the initial changes. As Dr Graham Watson, a colleague and longtime follower of the British Army noted to me: 'Following the unit changes in the British Army has become more difficult. After the relative openness of the *Army 2020* documents, there is now just a trickle of information. What seems to be happening is that some of the original decisions are being reversed.'

The Army's efforts to tinker with the changes being implemented would become referred to as *Army 2020 Refine* but, unlike the case for *Army 2020*, there would be little published material on these changes. However, *Army 2020 Refine* was not to continue as planned either. A completely new outlook appeared in March 2021 with publication of *Defence in a Competitive Age*. One section within that is titled 'Integrated Force 2030: Army'. These changes would in turn be replaced more recently by *Future Soldier*. Throughout this process I continued to look for information and my working document went through any number of iterations as news items, announcements, and other sources disclosed changes and as I added additional topics.

From 2010 onwards the government's defence policy was explicitly driven by the need to reduce the strength and cost of the armed forces, especially the Army. Each of the changes discussed in this book called for a reduction in the Army. In fact, reductions had begun even while the Army was still fighting in Iraq and Afghanistan. Operations in Iraq ended in July 2009; the Army did not cease combat operations and withdraw its last combat troops from Afghanistan until December 2014. The Strategic Defence and

Security Review had actually been published four years earlier, announcing plans for the elimination of units and personnel. This would be followed by the even smaller force in *Army 2020*.

Despite the continuing impetus of cuts based on budgets, this was not intended to simply be a series of reductions without thought. At each stage the government and Army made decisions about the threats the country would face and how the Army could be configured to meet them. This was not a consistent process, and there were periodic changes of direction and judgement on those issues. This entire progression did not go without criticism, with some alleging that the government oversold the Army's abilities to meet the demands it might face, or to accurately ascertain those demands in the first place. Many thought it unlikely, for example, that the new and lighter combat vehicles would actually be acquired until well after the changes that relied upon them had already been made (which indeed proved to be the case). For this reason, I have quoted extensively from various documents issued during the years covered by this work. It seemed only fair to allow the government to set out what they were planning, or hoping for, as much as possible in their own words.

Although containing background information going back to Options for Change in 1992–93, the major part of this work is a detailed examination of the British Army and its many changes from roughly 2010 into 2024.

In the discussion of formations in the main text (e.g., 3rd (UK) Division) the organisation shown is roughly that of 2020–21 or just before the *Future Soldier* changes began, although the intended changes are noted. Appendix IV (see Volume 2) shows the complete *Future Soldier* intended order of battle. Both in the text and in the Appendix, restructure dates are those in the original document, most of which were to have occurred in 2023. However, there is no good way to determine how many were made on time, or even when, and so the dates are shown as originally given to make clear what the plan was.

1 COMMAND

Army Command

British Army Headquarters is at Andover in north-west Hampshire. The senior officer is the Chief of the General Staff (CGS). This is the only four-star position in the Army itself, although full generals can also be found in inter-service or NATO positions. The incumbent is General Sir Roland (Roly) Walker KCB, DSO, appointed June 2024, succeeding General Sir Patrick Y. M. Sanders KCB, CBE, DSO, ADC Gen who was appointed in June 2022, who in turn succeeded General Sir Mark Carleton-Smith KCB, CBE, ADC Gen, who was appointed in June 2018. His predecessor, who oversaw much of the original *Army 2020* and *Army 2020 Refine* reorganisations, was General Sir Nicholas Patrick Carter KCB, CBE, DSO, ADC, who was appointed CGS in September 2014 and would then become Chief of the Defence Staff 2018–2021.

The CGS also has a small headquarters at the Ministry of Defence (MOD) in London, headed by the Assistant Chief of the General Staff, a major general position. There is now a Deputy CGS as well. From 2015–2019 it was Lieutenant General Sir Nicholas Pope KCB, CBE. He was succeeded 12 August 2019 by Lieutenant General Sir Christopher Tickell KBE (2021 Birthday Honours) and in August 2022 by Lieutenant General Dame Sharon P. M. Nesmith DCB (2024 New Years Honours), the Army's first female lieutenant general. She, in turn, would be replaced in June 2024 by Lieutenant General David J. Eastman MBE following her promotion to General and appointment as Vice Chief of the Defence Staff.

There are now two principal subordinate commands: Commander Field Army and Commander Home Forces.

The current Commander Field Army is Lieutenant General Michael R Elviss, CB, MBE appointed March 2024 to replace Lieutenant General Sir Ralph W. Wooddisse KCB (2022 Birthday Honours), CBE, MC appointed April 2021. The position was known as Commander Land Forces until November 2015. The CFA is in charge of most of the Army's operational elements at home or abroad: 1st (UK) Division, 3rd (UK) Division, 6th (UK) Division, and 16th Air Assault Brigade Combat Team. The CFA's chief of staff is located at Army Headquarters, serving as the principal contact there for the Assistant Chief of the General Staff. This HQ moved to Andover from Wilton near Salisbury in mid-2009.

Home Command actually began as the Adjutant General, restyled mid-2015 as Commander Personnel and Support. It was then redesignated Home Command in April 2016. The incumbent, from September 2023 is Lieutenant General Charles S. Collins DSO, MBE. His predecessor from June 2021 was Lieutenant General Ian J. Cave CB, formerly Chief of Staff, Field Army. Originally at Andover, this position is responsible for all aspects of personnel policy (such as recruiting, career management and personnel administration) as well as administrative functions (e.g., legal and medical services). The command HQ later moved to Aldershot. Home Command comprises Regional Command, London District, the Recruiting and Initial Training Command (formerly the Army Recruiting and Training Division), the Army Personnel Centre, and the Sandhurst Group [officer training]. Commander, Home Command is also the Standing Joint Commander (SJC(UK)), responsible for support to civil authorities in the UK.

Regional Command is a two-star position at Aldershot, responsible for stations and garrisons in the UK, Nepal and Brunei. It was formed November 2011 as Support Command, taking over interim administrative control of the various TA regional brigades as well as providing the lead on the Firm Base Concept. In 2015 it was renamed Regional Command and the various regional brigades were disbanded or amalgamated with Regular brigade and district headquarters. These serve as regional points of command (RPOCs), originally coming under 1st (UK) Division or Force Troops Command. These RPOCs are responsible for support of all units in their territory, Regular or Army Reserve, including university cadets. The Army's Firm Base Concept involves support for service personnel and veterans and 'partnership with agencies and organizations with statutory or moral obligations to deliver support to the defence community' according to *The British Army Journal* in 2011.

On 1 August 2019 several RPOCs transferred from 1st (UK) Division to Regional Command: HQ North West (Preston), HQ 38th

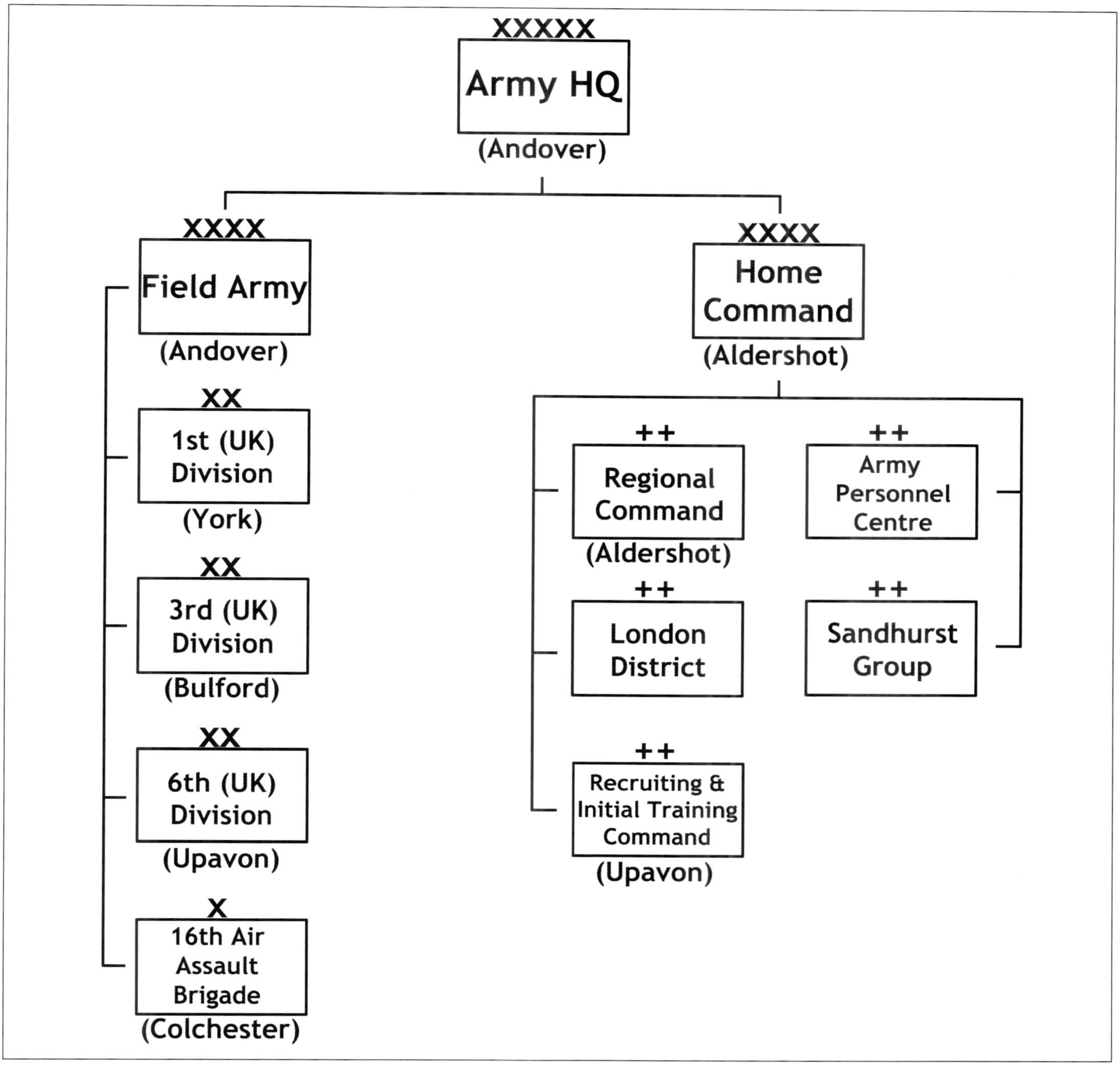

Structure of Army HQ. (Tom Cooper, based on author's diagram)

(Irish) Brigade (Lisburn) and HQ 160th (Welsh) Brigade (Brecon). The two brigades no longer controlled any infantry battalions or other units. A new HQ South West was formed at Tidworth after this was separated from HQ 1st Artillery Brigade and a new HQ West Midlands established at Donnington after that separated from 11th Signal Brigade; those brigades went to 3rd (UK) Division in 2019 and 2020. Under *Future Soldier*, the command will receive 51st Infantry Brigade and HQ Scotland from 1st (UK) Division, which will remain the RPOC for Scotland, giving up the currently assigned RAC and infantry. The various area HQs will be separated from 1st (UK) Division's brigades and transfer in as well. RPOC South East will remain at Aldershot and RPOC South West will remain at Tidworth. RPOCs North West and North East will combine as RPOC North, with its location still undetermined. RPOCs East Midlands and West Midlands will combine as RPOC Centre, based at Cottesmore with a Forward Node in the West Midlands.

In addition, in August 2019 Regional Command took over Provost Marshal (Army) and 1st Military Police Brigade from Force Troops Command. The brigade gave up the Royal Military Police (RMP) regiments to 101st Logistic Brigade of 3rd (UK) Division. It then comprised a variety of organisations such as the Special Investigation Branch Regiment, Military Provost Guard Service, and the Specialist Operations Regiment. These are discussed below in the section on the Royal Military Police under the Adjutant General's Corps.

London District is unique among the territorial headquarters in the UK in that it is a two-star command, with its headquarters at Whitehall. It is responsible for all Regular and Army Reserve units and cadet detachments within its area. It is perhaps best known for the various ceremonial events in London. Like Regional Command, it is now part of Home Command. It controls the Household Cavalry Mounted Regiment at Knightsbridge and the King's Troop RHA at

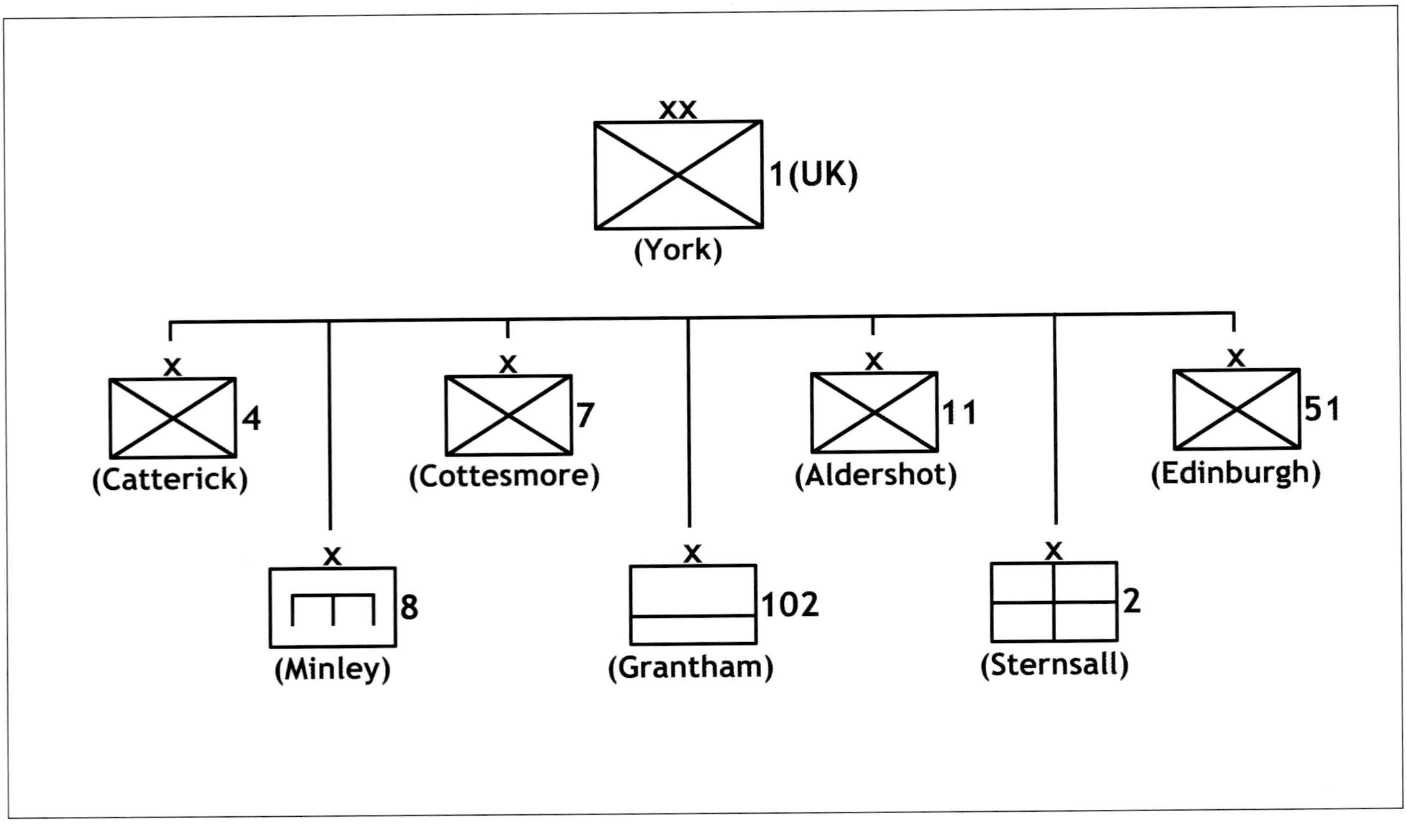

1st (UK) Division. (Tom Cooper, based on author's diagram)

Woolwich. It also has the public duties incremental companies of the Foot Guards regiments and the 1st Bn, London Guards [AR], along with 20 Logistic Support Squadron RLC and 238 (London) Signal Squadron. The four light role battalions of the Foot Guards alternate between light role, security force assistance and ceremonial duties in London, with one battalion at a time normally serving in the latter role. The GOC London District is concurrently the Major General commanding the Household Division.

HQ British Forces Germany (BFG) was formed in January 2012, replacing the prior United Kingdom Support Command (Germany). That HQ had been created in 1994 when British Army of the Rhine (BAOR) was disbanded. It moved from Rheindahlen to Bielefeld in summer 2013. HQ BFG provided support to all three armed services in Germany and elsewhere in Europe. One of its major tasks from 2013 was overseeing the departure of units from Germany under *Army 2020* and their rebasing in the United Kingdom. The position of Commander BFG was reduced to a one-star rank in 2015. The post lapsed the end of August 2019 when the last brigadier left. The final combat units departed for the UK that year. There is now a colonel known as Commander British Army Germany, responsible for the training area at Sennelager, storage facilities for heavy equipment (including tanks), and 23 Amphibious Engineer Squadron at Paderborn. Those Engineers, reduced to a troop under *Army 2020* and then reformed as a squadron in a joint British-German bridging battalion, are now the only formed British Army unit stationed in Germany.

Overview of Ministry of Defence and Defence Organisation

The Ministry of Defence is headed by the Defence Secretary, appointed by the Prime Minister. This role was created in 1964, along with the unified Ministry of Defence. There are currently four supporting Defence Ministers, all civilians. The senior civil servant is the Ministry of Defence Permanent Under Secretary. The senior military member (professional head of the armed forces) is the Chief of the Defence Staff. That position was created in 1959, before creation of the MOD itself. There is a Vice-Chief of the Defence Staff—usually of equivalent rank to the CDS but from a different service—and three deputies:

- Deputy Chief of Defence Staff (Military Strategy & Operations) (DCDS (MSO))
- Chief of Defence People (CDP)
- Deputy Chief of Defence Staff for Military Capability (DCDS (Mil Cap))

There are four military commands: the Royal Navy, the Royal Air Force, the Army, and Strategic Command, formerly Joint Forces Command.

There are 12 Enabling Organisations to provide a range of supporting services for the whole of MOD. Those most relevant to the Army are:

- Defence Equipment and Support (DE&S): Its purpose is to equip and support the UK's Armed Forces for current and future operations.
- Defence Digital: Defence Digital is the MOD's key organisation for the delivery of digital services and capabilities; it is positioned within Strategic Command.
- Defence Electronics and Components Agency (DECA): DECA is an executive agency and the MOD's principal electrical, electronic, avionic and general engineering organization for maintenance, repair, overhaul and upgrade deliveries.
- Defence Infrastructure Organisation (DIO): The DIO is the professional real estate expert for Defence, supporting the Armed Forces by enabling military capability through

The Household Cavalry Mounted Regiment, consisting of The Life Guards and The Blues and Royals, provide the Sovereign's Escort for public duties in London and are seen here participating in the King's Birthday Parade in June 2023. (APOLOND-OFFICIAL-20230610-058-062.jpg)

Cavalrymen of the Household Cavalry Mounted Regiment line the steps of the House of Lords at the State Opening of Parliament in November 2023. (APOLOND-OFFICIAL-20231107-095-371.jpg)

The King's Troop Royal Horse Artillery fire a 41 round King's Official Birthday Gun Salute after the parade in Green Park in June 2023. (KD1_5814.jpg)

The entrance to the Headquarters British Forces Germany (HQ BFG) at Herfeld, Bielefeld, seen in June 2013. (45156615.jpg)

planning, building, maintaining and servicing infrastructure: acquisition, operation, maintenance and disposition.

Ministry of Defence and Joint Commands (Military)

There is a Chief of the Defence Staff (CDS) at the Ministry of Defence. This individual is the professional head of the Armed Services and principal military advisor to the Secretary of State for Defence and the Prime Minister. The CDS coordinates the activities of the services through their professional heads: Chief of the Naval Staff and First Sea Lord, Chief of the General Staff, and Chief of the Air Staff. General Sir Nicholas Carter GCB, CBE, DSO, ADC Gen took over the post in June 2018; Carter had been Chief of the General Staff. General Carter was replaced in November 2021 by Admiral Sir Tony Radakin KCB, ADC. The Army's first female full general, Dame Sharon P. M. Nesmith DCB, was appointed as Vice Chief of the Defense Staff in June 2024.

The Headquarters, Joint Forces Command is at Northwood in Middlesex. JFC was made part of the Ministry of Defence, working to ensure that joint capabilities among the services are developed and maintained. They provide command and control for overseas operations. This is a four-star position, which has a Permanent Joint Headquarters (PJHQ) as well as a Directorate of Special Forces overseeing the various elements of United Kingdom Special Forces (UKSF). They also have support elements (including the Defence Academy, information systems, and the Surgeon General). JFC was in charge of the Permanent Joint Operating Bases (PJOBs) overseas such as those in Cyprus and the South Atlantic. They were also in control of the Joint Counter Terrorism Training and Advisory Team and Joint Arms Control Implementation Team. The command reached initial operating capability in April 2012 and full operating capability in April 2013. General Sir Patrick Sanders KCB (2020 Honours List), CBE, DSO ADC Gen (the former Commander Field Army) took command in May 2019. The immediately available combat force is known as the Joint Rapid Reaction Force (JRRF). The Army's 16th Air Assault Brigade and the Royal Marines' 3rd Commando Brigade are the core elements, supported by the Joint Helicopter Command and the Royal Navy's Response Task Group.

The Defence Secretary announced in July 2019 that JFC would be transformed into Strategic Command: 'we must have strategic integration across the five warfighting domains – land, air, sea, space and cyber.' Strategic Command will oversee the military digital information network and was to cooperate with UK allies in space. It will continue to have responsibility for a range of strategic and defence-wide capabilities and oversight of the UK military's global footprint and 'continue enabling our operations and providing critical advice on force development.' The redesignation occurred in December 2019. *Defence in a Competitive Age* noted that Strategic Command:

> is at the heart of confronting the myriad threats we now face. Driving integration across all domains. Strategic Command will ensure we join up the people, the equipment and the information, and deliver our outputs in a more sophisticated way – from space, in the skies, on land, at sea, or in cyberspace – making the whole force more than the sum of its parts.

It would 'provide the platform for our armed forces to shift to a more dynamic and competitive posture' and 'continuously experiment and innovate with technology to ensure we maintain operational advantage.' Responsibility for space was later transferred from Strategic Command to the new UK Space Command, established 1 April 2021. It is also a joint command, although it 'sits' under the RAF.

The Permanent Joint Headquarters was established in April 1996 as a three-star position, becoming part of the new Joint Forces Command when that formed. Its head is designated as the Chief of Joint Operations. The CJO plans for and commands UK forces assigned for specific overseas operations. 250 (Gurkha) Signal Squadron at Bramcote, Nuneaton provides command support when Commander Joint Forces Operations is deployed. Lt Gen [RM] Sir Charles Strickland KCB, OBE took over in November 2021 from Vice Admiral Benjamin [Ben] Key CBE who had held the role since April 2019.

The Joint Helicopter Command (JHC) is a two-star position, with command rotating among the services. It was established in 1999 and has control over all of the battlefield support and lift helicopters of the Army, Royal Air Force and Royal Navy. The HQ is co-located with Army HQ at Andover. In addition to the helicopter squadrons, JHC formerly had operational control of 16th Air Assault Brigade. As noted, in November 2015 that brigade was transferred to the direct command of HQ Field Army. An Army major general was in command 2014–2017, succeeded by a rear admiral, and then (March 2020) an air vice marshal.

In 2014 NATO created the Very High Readiness Joint Task Force (VJTF), with units on standby for rapid deployment if necessary. Its first deployment was in 2022 following the Russian invasion of Ukraine. Leadership is rotated annually among NATO members; the UK assumed lead 1 January 2024 with 7th Light Mechanised Brigade taking on the role. The VJTF has around 6,000 personnel, with a light cavalry regiment, four light mechanised infantry battalions, artillery, tanks, helicopters and supporting service units. Current British units are the Royal Scots Dragoon Guards and 2nd Bn Royal Anglian Regiment. The brigade is supposed to be ready to deploy within days. NATO's Joint Force Command in Brunssum will command the Response Force in 2024. Nine countries contribute to the VJTF in addition to the UK. However, this force probably lapsed later in 2024 with creation of the Allied Reaction Force: see 1st (UK) Division.

2
ARMY 2020 AND *ARMY 2020 REFINE*

The Path to *Army 2020* and *Army 2020 Refine*

The British Army underwent a major reorganisation and restructuring in 1992–1993 (Options for Change) following the end of the Cold War. The result was a deployable division HQ in Germany (1st (UK) Armoured Division), with three armoured brigades (4th, 7th and 20th), and a deployable division HQ in the UK (3rd (UK) Division), also with three brigades (two mechanised – 1st and 19th – and one airborne – 5th). There was also an independent airportable infantry brigade (24th). In 1999 the airborne and airportable brigades were partially merged and combined with AAC regiments to form the 16th Air Assault Brigade. A third mechanised brigade (12th) was then formed to complete the UK-based division. The Army also provided the artillery and engineers for the Royal Marines' 3rd Commando Brigade.

Following the 2003 invasion of Iraq, the British provided a brigade for the continuing struggle, each serving on a six-month roulement tour (Operation Telic). This continued until the final tour ended in April 2009. The mechanised brigade from Germany moved to the UK after a tour in Iraq ended in June 2008. Beginning in May 2006 the British also provided a brigade for the war in Afghanistan (Operation Herrick). These were also six-month tours, and finally ended in December 2014.

The Army did not undergo any major structural changes during this time, although the number of regiments with tanks were reduced, with a Germany-based brigade (4th) changed to mechanised and a UK-based brigade (19th) changed to light. This was part of a process known as *Future Army Structure* (FAS), announced by the CGS 16 December 2004. The future size of the Army would be set at 102,000 and there would be a reduction in the number of infantry battalions as various regiments were consolidated. Another change was the realignment of existing Volunteer infantry units as numbered battalions of infantry regiments. For example, the East of England Regiment would become 3rd (V) Bn The Royal Anglian Regiment, the West Midlands Regiment would become 4th (V) Bn The Mercian Regiment, and the 52nd Lowland Volunteers would become the 6th (V) Bn of the new Royal Regiment of Scotland. This was the same time that formation of The Royal Regiment of Scotland and The Rifles as new regiments was announced. There was some restructuring in the other arms and services as well.

As part of FAS, the Army began to phase out the Arms Plot: shifting units from station to station and sometimes altering their roles. This meant that infantry battalions and RAC regiments would now remain at one station except when sent on short unaccompanied tours, known in the British Army as roulement (rolling) tours, usually six months or less. In addition they would no longer re-role from one establishment to another: e.g., light role infantry to armoured infantry. Withdrawal from Germany – a major goal of *Army 2020* – would largely eliminate the need for units based overseas. Under *Army 2020* only the Foot Guards would continue a form of the Arms Plot, with battalions (but not their families) rotating among five locations in the UK, with three different roles (ceremonial, light role infantry and more recently security force assistance). The Scots Guards, mechanised, remained apart from that scheme.

In 2010, the government undertook an examination of how to 'be more thoughtful, more strategic and more coordinated in the way we advance our interests and protect our national security.' However, this look had to also find a way to cut the defence budget: 'bringing the defence budget back to balance is a vital part of how we tackle the deficit and protect this country's national security.' The resulting document was known as the *Strategic Defence and Security Review* (SDSR), issued in October 2010. Since this looked at all of the armed forces, the desirable goal was dubbed *Future Force 2020*: it was assumed that achieving this future state could take up to 10 years. The remaining forces in Germany were to be withdrawn, with the Army having five multi-role brigades along with 16th Air Assault Brigade. There would be a further reduction in tanks, heavier armoured vehicles and artillery with new and

British Mastiff armoured vehicles on patrol during Operation Charge of the Knights-14 in Basrah City, with the UK Military Transition Team (MITT) Group attached to 50 Brigade, Iraqi Army in June 2008. (45149762.jpg)

A night vision image of a soldier from the Duke of Wellington's Regiment taking up a fire position ready to start Operation Gray Wolf near Sharkarta, Iraq in 2005. (45150513.jpg)

A corporal from the Royal Artillery provides covering fire while members of 4 Brigade Reconnaissance Force cross open ground on Operation QALB. Op QALB was a joint ISAF and ANSF operation, its aim was to find enemy caches and disturb Insurgent supply chains. (45154935.jpg)

Royal Engineers from 44 HQ and Support Squadron installing a General Support Bridge (GSB) in the northern part of Nahr-e Seraj District of Helmand Province in 2012. (45156344.jpg)

lighter armoured vehicles to be developed. There would be a single deployable division HQ, with another one geared for training and preparing units for operations, capable (with suitable warning and augmentation) of deploying if need be. By 2015, the Army would decrease from 102,000 to around 95,000. There was to be a separate study of the reserve forces.

While SDSR was an attempt to analyse threats and resources, with some retrenchment, it was never implemented. The government's determination to make deeper defence cuts led to what was called *Army 2020*. This new scheme was announced in July 2012. While nominally the Army's intent to meet the direction first set out in the SDSR, it called for a much smaller Army, albeit one designed to be 'a more adaptable and flexible Army, capable of undertaking a broader range of military tasks….' The Army would now be reduced to 82,000 men by 2020, although this would be supplemented by an increased and improved Reserve element of 30,000. The intended closer integration of Regular and Reserve forces will be discussed below.

The Army would be divided between the Reaction Force and the Adaptable Force. The Reaction Force would provide units able to undertake short notice contingency tasks as well as conventional deterrence. It would have a division HQ, three armoured infantry brigades, and 'associated enablers'. Given their role, about 90 percent of the strength would be Regulars. The Adaptable Force would have a non-deployable division HQ and the various combat units not part of the Reaction Force. The bulk of the artillery, engineers, and support and service troops would be in brigades under Force Troops Command. Further details were contained in a July 2013 update. This repeated the idea of integrating the Reserves into the force structure by design, so that they could be 'used routinely, not just in extreme circumstances.' The underlying budget-driver for this whole process was actually put in the document: 'The UK's economic climate remains a strategic threat to the nation, which means that cost and efficiency must remain a vital driver in force design and optimizing capability'. This update also set out formation basing. There was a detailed presentation of the units in the Reaction Force, Adaptable Force and Force Troops Command as well as a discussion of the transition and training cycles.

In 2013 the US RAND Corporation issued a report on *Setting Priorities in the Age of Austerity*, looking at the British, French, and German experiences.[1] It suggested that *Army 2020* was a plan for 'substantially recasting the British Army's mission, its approach to readiness, and its force structure.' SDSR had already called for cutting Army strength and reducing MBT and AS90 (155mm SP howitzer) strength. The Army was counting on new, lighter vehicles to be their backbone, even though actual acquisition would be delayed into the next decade. As we know now, these future vehicles have not yet arrived (at the time of writing), Ajax and Boxer being prime examples. The US study felt that the British excluded any possibility of war against a peer enemy, and that the troops in the Reaction Force might be the only part of the Army with conventional fighting skills. Finally, the British seemed to assume that they would not need to sustain a brigade-sized force for any period of time, i.e., no more Afghanistans. Near the end, the study noted the danger 'that the UK will be hampered by aging equipment while it waits for its modernisation programs to regain lost ground.' As we will see, this would prove true. In their conclusion they felt that the British Army was in the worst state of the three studied, given how Iraq and

AS90 155mm self-propelled howitzers firing during Exercise Steel Sabre in January 2014. (45158544.jpg)

Afghanistan had strained their resources especially in the face of successive budget cuts.

The report on the review of the Reserve forces had been issued back in July 2011 under the title *Future Reserves 2020*. Its conclusion was that the 'UK's Reserve Forces are in need of significant revitalisation and re-orientation'. They also felt that the Reserves formed too small a portion of overall military capability. Key conclusions were that the Reserve forces were in decline; their roles had not been modernised; their potential (i.e., their voluntary ethos) was not being fully exploited; and that the Reserves were not being used efficiently. While *Army 2020* called for a Reserve force built up to 30,000 personnel, the Review noted that trained and active strength at the time was estimated at only 14,000 personnel against an establishment of 37,000. Territorial Army units were understrength, with aging personnel, and subject to a 2009 freeze on their training and pay, later reversed. The conclusions noted earlier also indicated the nature of the recommendations. These included not only improving training and equipment but consolidating the many small sub-units into fewer centres to allow better unit cohesion and training. They also looked at pay and other issues that would affect recruitment and retention, as well as the integration of the Reserves into a cohesive and integrated Whole Force structure.

In October 2012, the government announced that the Territorial Army was to be renamed the Army Reserve. This was intended to emphasise their role as an 'integral part' of the Army with the same kit and equipment as the Regulars and increased training with the full-time soldiers and pairing of Regular and Reserve units. As part of this effort, the parenthetical '(Volunteers)' was removed from all of their unit titles. As *Army 2020* was implemented 2013–2015, there was an increase in the number of hybrid units (mixed Regular and AR) and an effort to pair Regular and Army Reserve units. The announced 2012 name change to Army Reserve only became legal in May 2014 with the Defence Reform Act of 2014.

Combat Capability for the Future from late 2013 even noted that Reserves might be providing full platoons to each rifle company as well as augmentation to other elements of each light protected mobility battalion during training exercises and operational deployments and that light role infantry battalions would likewise have an integrated Army Reserve platoon in each company as well as other Reserve elements. It does not appear that AR platoons were ever embedded in Regular units. However, composite AR companies have served in Iraq, Afghanistan, and (in a reduced battalion strength) a tour under the UN on Cyprus. A composite Yeomanry squadron has served in the Baltic. With the changes under *Army 2020 Refine* and later, the number of hybrid units has actually been reduced.

One goal of *Army 2020* was to bring the Army home from Germany. There were up to 16,000 soldiers there at the beginning of the process, and the last elements finally departed in 2019. Returning troops and their families to the UK, as well as the movement of units and families within the UK itself, required a major effort to erect the necessary housing and base infrastructure. One 2013 estimate was that these measures could cost £1.8 billion by 2020.

As mentioned, *Army 2020* had not even been fully implemented when the government began looking to further downsize and reorganise the Armed Forces: *National Security Strategy and Strategic Defence and Security Review 2015: A Secure and Prosperous United Kingdom* (November 2015). Here again, the real aim is given

A Challenger 2 tank of the Queens Royal Lancers, attached to the 1st Royal Regiment of Fusiliers (1 RRF) Battlegroup, demonstrates its ability to the world's media, at Camp Coyote, Kuwait in March 2003, photographed a few days before the launch of Operation Telic. (45142648.jpg)

A soldier from of 73 Engineer Regiment taking part in a battle exercise in 2008, carries out personal decontamination drills to protect himself from chemical agents. The exercise focused on chemical defence training. (45150769.jpg)

away in the title: not a secure United Kingdom, but a 'secure and prosperous' United Kingdom. The first two sentences in the Prime Minister's Foreword to the document are: 'Our national security depends on our economic security, and vice versa. So the first step in our National Security Strategy is to ensure our economy is, and remains, strong.'

In its early stages, *Army 2020 Refine* aimed to change the Army's main combat force from three armoured infantry brigades to two much smaller armoured infantry brigades and two new strike brigades. Apparently, 'strike' sounded more impressive than 'mechanised', which is what the new brigades actually were. 16th Air Assault Brigade was still retained outside the division structure, but initial plans to reduce it from three to two battalions were later reversed. There would also be some reshuffling of unit assignments and roles, and some disbanding and reorganisation of Regular Army and Army Reserve units. What would become much more extensive changes under *Defence in a Competitive Age* and *Future Soldier* will be discussed below.

Defence in a Competitive Age

In March 2021 the government produced a document titled *Defence in a Competitive Age*. Issued by the Secretary of State for Defence; this was intended 'to seek out and to understand future threats, and to invest in the capabilities to defeat them.' While addressing all services, one intention was to have the Army 'more deployed and better protected.' There was a specific section on 'Integrated Force 2030: Army.' In theory, the Army would receive 'an additional £3 billion in new Army equipment on top of the more than £20 billion planned. Investment in new vehicles (including Ajax, Boxer and Challenger 3); modernised long-range precision fires (including multiple launched [sic] rocket systems and Apache helicopters); new air defences; tactical surveillance drones; and new electronic warfare and cyberspace capabilities….' However, personnel strength

A soldier from A Company 3rd Battalion The Parachute Regiment, gives fire support from a GPMG (General Purpose Machine Gun) during a training exercise. Troops from the 3rd Battalion The Parachute Regiment Battle Group conducted Exercise Grand Prix 5 in Kenya in 2010. (45151822.jpg)

would be cut from the current effective strength of 76,000 to 72,500 by 2025. Before looking at their view of operational combat brigades, the Review noted that the 'creation of Combat Service Support Battalions will require fewer separate units of logisticians, electrical and mechanical engineers, and medics.' The infantry would lose one battalion (identified separately as 2nd Bn The Mercian Regiment) while another (later identified as 2nd Bn The Royal Yorkshire Regiment) would be turned into an experimental battalion, to try out new equipment and how it could be integrated into units.

The Army would have seven combat brigades: two heavy (later identified as 12th and 20th Armoured), two light (since identified as 4th Light and 7th Light Mechanised), one air manoeuvre (16th Air Assault), the new 1st Combat Aviation Brigade, and the new 1st Deep Reconnaissance Strike Brigade. The last was described in the document as an 'Army fighting formation for executing long-range strike and reconnaissance activities.' It began forming in summer 2022 from elements of the disbanded 1st Armoured Infantry and 1st Artillery Brigades. The heavy brigades would form from the current 12th and 20th Armoured Infantry Brigades. Each would have an Ajax regiment (recce), an armoured regiment with the Challenger 3, and two Boxer mechanised battalions. The strike brigades were to be abandoned.

There would be a new Army Special Operations Brigade with the new Ranger Regiment (four battalions), built around personnel from the four UK battalions of the Specialised Infantry Group. Each of the Ranger battalions would have 250 personnel, and ultimately they would draw personnel from throughout the Army. The new regiment was to stand up in August 2021 (later changed to December 2021), and the hope was that it would be fully operational in 2022. The Army Special Operations Brigade would replace the Specialised Infantry Group, with soldiers taking on roles usually carried out by special forces personnel: training, advising and accompanying allies in high threat environments.

There would also be a new Security Force Assistance Brigade; 11th Infantry Brigade became the 11th Security Force Assistance Brigade in late 2021 and was expected to reorganise beginning the following year. It appears that this brigade will take on the tasks originally intended for the Specialised Infantry Group: units and personnel deployed around the world to build the capacity of allied and partner nations by providing guidance and training. The term and concept are copied from the US Army, which activated its first security force assistance brigade in 2018. The US brigades have about 800 personnel and are designed to carry out 'train, advise and assist' missions with foreign military partners. Unlike the new British brigade, the US brigades consist only of officers and NCOs, all volunteers. They were formed to relieve combat brigades of the combat advisory mission.

Future Soldier

Army 2020, *Army 2020 Refine* and *Defence in a Competitive Age* have now been replaced by *Future Soldier*. This calls for '[a]n expeditionary Army ready for the next challenge, not the last.' A detailed overview of this plan was published in November 2021 as *The Future Soldier Guide*. This was billed as the most radical transformation of the Army in 20 years:

> Future Soldier is about delivering a modern British Army that is fit for the challenges of the future. To become more lethal, agile and expeditionary; an army able to fight and win wars and to compete successfully in the grey-zone between peace and war. An army equipped with the right culture and leadership to sustain our reputation and moral foundation, and to make the Army a great place to be, for everyone. An army ready for the future, not the past.

The AJAX prototype shown near its assembly site in Merthyr Tydfil, Wales in March 2016. AJAX is intended to provide a step-change in the armoured fighting vehicle capability being delivered to the British Army. The programme includes six variants: AJAX, ARES, APOLLO, ATHENA, ATLAS and ARGUS. At the time of writing the project has had a much-troubled history and the vehicles have yet to enter operational service. (45159443.jpg)

The 2019 Army Combat Power Demonstration (ACPD) took place on Salisbury Plain from 28 – 30 October 2019. Visitors saw the next generation of armoured vehicles with both Ajax and Boxer (pictured) providing an insight into how the Army's Strike capability in the future was intended to look. (DES-2019-251-004.jpg)

A soldier from the Ranger Regiment poses with the new Alternative Individual Weapons (AIW) system at Lulworth Training area in July 2023. (AHQCPL12-OFFICIAL-20230713-015-013.jpg)

As hinted but not explicitly stated in *Defence in a Competitive Age*, *Future Soldier* made clear that 1st (UK) Division would be an operational division again, with (possibly) deployable brigade combat teams (4th Light and 7th Light Mechanised) along with the security force assistance brigade (11th). Its brigades would shed their RPOC roles as area HQs and a new brigade (19th) would be formed to take control of some AR units. 3rd (UK) and 6th (UK) Divisions would also be reorganised. 3rd (UK) Division would have two armoured brigade combat teams (12th and 20th) and the new 1st Deep Recce Strike Brigade Combat Team. 6th (UK) Division, although largely changed, would continue to be a 'holding company' for various units: 'the home of our unconventional warfare capabilities'. The new brigade combat teams would include some of their supporting services – especially RLC and REME – as integral parts, rather than having them controlled by another HQ in peacetime. This makes them more like the 16th Air Assault Brigade Combat Team, which always had full control over its supporting units.

The intent was to make the Army more global in perspective, operations and partnerships. 'The Army will be balanced to deliver right across the Defence spectrum: Protect the Homeland; Engage with allies and partners overseas; Constrain the aggressive activities of our adversaries; and Fight wars if required.' It appears that 3rd (UK) Division is now intended for operations as a complete division against a comparable (peer) enemy force, in a NATO context, while 1st (UK) Division would not operate as a formation, but possibly at up to brigade level in low intensity environments.

When considering the war in Ukraine, according to an August 2022 article in *The Economist*, the CGS announced that the British Army would, in the future, 'major in urban combat'. The article went on to discuss how fighting in cities negates much of the technology (including satellite navigation and drones) Western armies rely on. At the same time, this can make cities a type of sanctuary from the enemy's ability to use the same kind of technologies against them. According to the article, Major General James Bowder (then Director of Futures, Army Command), said that the British Army has been analysing what the opening battles of a war between NATO and Russia would look like in view of experience in Ukraine. This may affect training, but it is hard to see how 3rd (UK) Division is really suited for the type of warfare occurring in Ukraine. The then CGS also noted, on the BBC in June 2022, that Russia's invasion of Ukraine underlines the Army's core purpose – to protect the UK and to be ready to fight and win wars on land – and reinforces the requirement to deter Russian aggression with the threat of force. He further noted his goal to 'accelerate the mobilisation and modernisation of the Army to reinforce Nato [sic] and deny Russia the chance to occupy any more of Europe… we are the generation that must prepare the Army to fight in Europe once again'. Another *Economist* article, from May 2023, noted that the British Army might have only eight days, or less, of munitions in stock and it was not clear if it could actually field one heavy division.

As with prior plans, the Army Reserve was to become better trained and more closely integrated with the Regular Army: 'more capable, more ready and more usable….' However, it may well be the case that their main purpose will be to continue providing trained replacements or augmentation to Regular units. Finally, there would be better training and equipment for the Army. The planned *Future Soldier* order of battle is contained in Appendix IV (see Volume 2).

A somewhat critical overview of the new directions for the Army by Dr Simon Anglim in October 2021 concluded that:

> Rather than "the best little army in the world", it might be more accurate to describe the British Army as a small army with some world-class capabilities (in line with some of our European allies) and some of those capabilities are going to be very stretched indeed if the Army follows the pattern laid out for it in these proposals. While the British Army is often accused of preparing for the last war, in this case, it seems to be trying to avoid it….

The allusion is presumably to Afghanistan as the last war, perhaps along with Iraq.

The *Integrated Review Refresh 2023*, according to the Prime Minister's introduction, was intended to take account of the geopolitical changes that had occurred since the 2021 *Integrated Review*. This included COVID-19, Russia's invasion of Ukraine, and China's increasing aggressiveness, along with long-standing threats from terrorism and organised crime. 'The 2023 refresh therefore builds on the approach set out in the *Integrated Review*, setting out the next evolutionary step in delivering on its aims, against the backdrop of a more volatile and contested world.' It sets out four pillars to this updated IR strategic framework:

- 'Shape the international environment'
- 'Deter, defend and compete across all domains'
- 'Address vulnerabilities through resilience'
- 'Generate strategic advantage'

Throughout the discussion in the document, there is almost nothing addressing any problems or concern with the equipment, strength or orientation of the Army. Of the £5 billion in new money for defence, £3 billion would go to the defence nuclear enterprise and

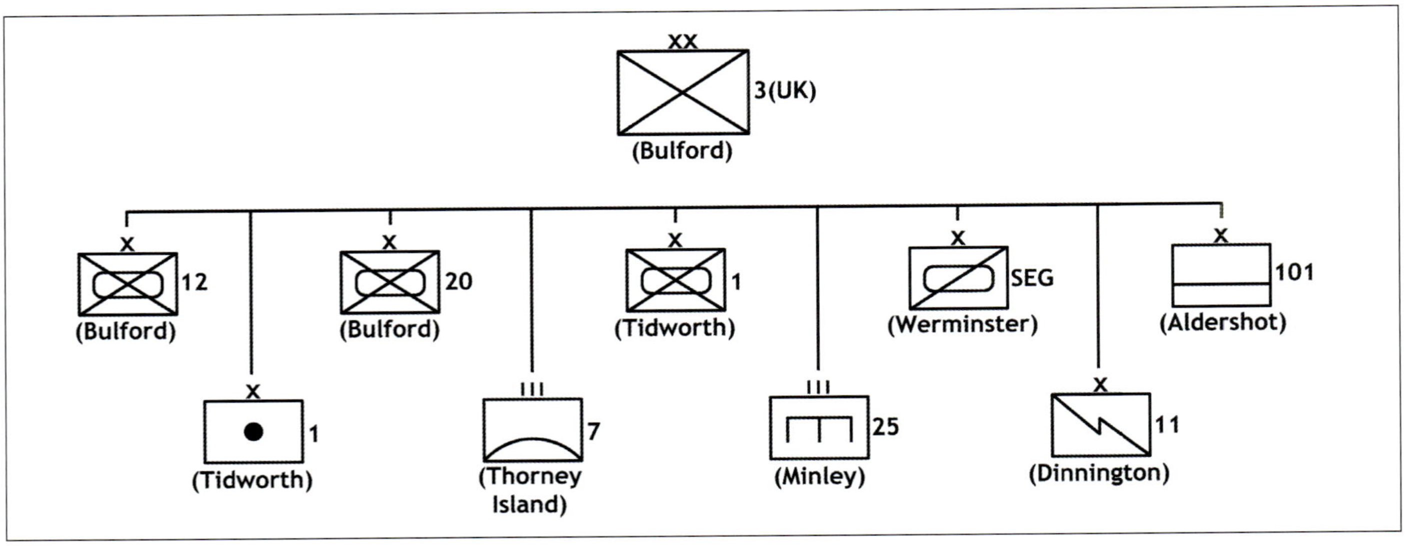

3rd (UK) Division. (Tom Cooper, based on author's diagram)

the rest to replenish and increase stockpiles, on top of a prior £560 million announced in autumn 2022. Thus, the Army might receive little more than additional monies for munitions.

This was followed in July 2023 by yet another integrated review, termed *Defence's response to a more contested and volatile world*. The Ministerial Foreword began: '[w]e did not plan on issuing a new Command Paper just two years since the last, but we have gone from a competitive age to a contested and volatile world.' The reference 'last' is to *Defence in a Competitive Age*. The war in Ukraine made clear that Russia was the country's primary threat, and the purpose of the new paper is 'on how to drive the lessons of Ukraine into our core business and to recover the warfighting resilience needed to generate credible conventional deterrence.'

There is nothing Army-specific in this document, in terms of planned organisation and equipment. However, the Army would benefit from plans to broaden the appeal of military service, its terms and conditions, and care of service families and veterans. This could include 'zig-zag' careers where someone is in the military for, say, six years and then leaves for other desired employment before returning for an additional period in service. They would also consider increasing lateral entry for those well into their careers. The document notes that the war in Ukraine makes clear that 'Reserves are essential both on and off the battlefield.' Thus the government will need to enhance the way that Reserves are supported. There is also a recognition that modern warfare requires greater acquisition of munitions as well as ensuring that industry can provide that support. This would include improving the speed of procurement. Part of this will include 'prioritising timely delivery over perfection.' There needed to be a better review of holdings of expendable items as well as increased investment in holding facilities. The commitment to NATO 'is ironclad and unwavering' and the Army will continue to lead the multinational Enhanced Forward Presence Battlegroup in Estonia. The Army will also offer to strengthen, with its allies, the ARRC 'as a strategic reserve for NATO's land forces.' Since the ARRC does not have any assigned combat units in peacetime, this would appear to confirm other reports that 3rd (UK) Division is indeed intended for service with ARRC in case of conflict.

A Trident II D5 Missile breaking the surface, having been fired from HMS *Vanguard*, a Strategic Missile Submarine in 2006. (45145143.jpg)

3
THE BRITISH ARMY IN THE 2020s

Personnel Strength

The Army on 1 January 2023 had 113,940 personnel as shown in Table 1. Other Personnel includes the Serving Regular Reserve,[2] Sponsored Reserve,[3] Military Provost Guard Service, Locally Engaged Personnel, and elements of the Full-Time Reserve Service (FTRS). The latter are reservists who apply for full time positions in certain selected postings for limited periods of time. The total strength is some 8,000 below the strength in January 2021.

Of the Regular Forces, 72,480 (96.4 percent) are trained and 69,190 (92.0 percent) are trade trained. Of the 26,240 in the Volunteer Reserve, 24,130 are trained.

Table 1: Army Personnel Strength 1 January 2023 and 1 January 2024

	2023	2024
Regular Forces	78,060	75,170
Gurkhas	4,060	4,060
Volunteer Reserve	27,570	26, 240
Other Personnel	4,250	4,560
Total	113,940	110,030

From 1 October 2016 personnel who had completed Phase 1 training (basic Service training) but not Phase 2 training (trade training) were considered trained; once they complete Phase 2 they are trade trained – which had been the prior definition of trained.

The goal under *Army 2020* was 82,000 Regular and 30,000 Army Reserve personnel. The 2015 defence review vowed to maintain the 82,000 strength. Elimination of a number of Regular Army units and headquarters under *Army 2020 Refine* was intended to free up those personnel to strengthen the remaining units. However, some of those planned rationalisations (Army speak for disbanding) have been postponed or cancelled. In any case, neither the Regular or Army Reserve strength goal is being maintained.

The Ministry of Defence documents from which these figures have been extracted do not separate the Royal Marines from the Royal Navy as a whole, and there are no separate figures for the RAF Regiment in the RAF data.

The most recent figures give the Royal Marines 5,820 Regulars as of 1 April 2022. The Royal Marine Reserve may only have some 600 personnel.

The RAF Regiment in March 2021, again using unofficial figures, had 1,850 Regular personnel; in 2016 there were 570 reservists.

Key Items of Equipment

The information in Table 2 is taken from *UK armed forces equipment and formations*, 9 September 2021 and 11 October 2022 versions. Numbers are as of 1 April 2021 and 1 April 2022. The documents have figures for 2016–2021 for most items. Initial figures here are for 2021. The version of the document for 2023 lacks the detail of the earlier documents, providing only some general figures.

An Apache AH1 helicopter from 4 Regiment, 656 Squadron Army Air Corps, during live firing training at Otterburn Ranges in Northumberland in 2009. (45150281.jpg)

Table 2: Key Items of Equipment 2021–2022		
Item	**Quantity**	**Notes**
Armoured Fighting Vehicles		
Challenger 2 MBT	227	unchanged since 2016, same in 2022
CVR(T) Scimitar	179	down from 181 the prior year and 201 before that, 170 in 2022
Warrior	767	down from 769 in prior years, 770 in 2016, 721 in 2022
Ajax	19 in 2021 21 in 2022	
Total	1,192 in 2021 1,139 in 2022	The Warrior was moved into this category in 2021, having previously been grouped with armoured personnel carriers. The 2023 report shows 625 Warrior AFVs but no details on the other vehicles.
Protected Mobility Vehicles		
Coyote	72	up from 71 in prior years, same in 2022
Foxhound	398	unchanged, same in 2022
Husky	218	down from 311, 2022 reduced to 0
Jackal	437	unchanged, 431 in 2022
Mastiff	396	unchanged; peak in 2016 was 421, 387 in 2022
Ridgeback	168	unchanged, 164 in 2022
Wolfhound	125	unchanged, 99 in 2022
Total	1,814 in 2021 1,551 in 2022	
Armoured Personnel Carriers		
Viking	99	unchanged; same in 2022. Only used by the Royal Marines.
Bulldog [FV432]	880	down from 891; peak in 2016 was 895, 851 in 2022. The 2023 report shows 746 Bulldog APCs.
Total	979 in 2021 950 in 2022	
Artillery		
AS90 155mm SP Gun	89	unchanged, same in 2022
L118 105mm Light Gun	126	unchanged, same in 2022
MLRS	35	unchanged, 29 in 2022
Total	250 in 2021 244 in 2022	The 2023 report shows 212 artillery pieces, without providing any details.
Combat Engineering Equipment		
M3 Amphibius Vehicle	27	down from 35; had been 37 until 2019, still 27 in 2022
Terrier	56	had been 60 until 2019, same in 2022
Titan	33	unchanged, same in 2022
Trojan	32	unchanged, same in 2022
		The 2023 report shows 148 engineering equipment pieces without providing any details.
Combat Support Equipment		
Wheeled Support Vehicles	7,009	down from 7,264, 6,781 in 2022
Landrovers	6,756	down from 7,595, 6,609 in 2022
Heavy Equipment Transporter	182	unchanged, same in 2022
Wheeled Tanker (Tractor)	356	up from 355, 354 in 2022
Wheeled Tanker (Trailer)	432	up from 431, same in 2022
		The documents only have data beginning in 2020 for combat support equipment. Wheeled support vehicles are 6t, 8t and 15t.
Rotary-Wing Aircraft		
Apache AH1	30	28 in service. Down from 50 in 2019 and 42 in 2020, 20 in 2022 (18 in service)
Apache AH-64E	16	4 in service, new 2022.
AW109SP	1	unchanged, 2022 still 1 but none in service
Bell 212	5	all in service; unchanged, 3 in 2022 (all in service). Based in Brunei; the AAC squadron there was disbanded in 2022 and replaced by an RAF flight with Pumas.

Chinook	60	41 in service; unchanged, 59 in 2022 (41 in service)
Gazelle	26	19 in service; down from 32 (but still only 19 in service) in 2019, 17 in 2022 (14 in service)
Merlin Mk3/3a/4/4a	25	12 in service; down from 21 in service, same in 2022
Puma HC2	23	17 in service; unchanged, 17 in 2022, 14 in service
Wildcat AH1	34	25 in service; unchanged, same in 2022
A5365 Dauphin 2	6	2 in 2022, both in service. Used by 658 Squadron AAC in support of special forces
		The documents do not break helicopters down by service, but it is fairly easy to determine those that would be under Joint Helicopter Command or special forces. Training helicopters used by the Army and RAF have been excluded. The 2023 report shows a total of 294 rotary-wing platforms, without providing any breakdown. Of the 258 for which details were known to the MOD, 193 (75%) were in service.
Unmanned Aircraft Systems		
Desert Hawk III	229	all in service, 229 still in 2022 but 228 in service
Watchkeeper	46	11 in service in 2021, 47 in 2022 (13 in service); peak strength had been 50
		On 1 April 2023 the UK had 194 unmanned aircraft systems in total, mainly due to the planned retirement of the Desert Hawk III.

Notable in Table 2 is the wind-down of the original Apache AH1 fleet and the beginnings of its replacement by the new AH-64E. The Army began buying 50 AH-64Es from the US in January 2022, and the first 14 entered service with 3rd Regiment AAC. The regiment was operational by autumn 2022. The last 36 aircraft are expected by summer 2024. This would end up restoring the prior strength of 50 and completely replacing the Apache AH1. Each regiment will have 18 Apaches.

There are four Wildcat squadrons (three Army and one Navy), meaning that they average six helicopters in service per squadron; this is known to be the establishment for the Army squadrons. The three Chinook squadrons in the RAF would average around 14 aircraft each in service, and their two Puma squadrons around eight each in service. The number needed for the OCU or training is unknown, so it might be somewhat fewer for each. The two RN Merlin squadrons would seem to have, like the Wildcat units, only six aircraft each in service.

For comparison, the combat aviation brigade in a US division normally contains three battalions. The attack/recce battalion has 24 AH-64 Apaches; the assault helicopter battalion has 30 UH-60 Black Hawks; and the general support aviation battalion has eight UH-60 command helicopters, 12 CH-47 Chinooks, and 15 HH-60 Black Hawks (medevac helicopters). The US Army also has non-divisional aviation brigades and units which can supplement the divisional brigades.

The British Army's new Apache AH-64E attack helicopter spearheading the deployment of helicopters on NATO's largest military exercise since the Cold War on 24 April 2024. 4 Regiment Army Air Corps Battlegroup (4 AAC BG) – a potent and capable mix of Army Air Corps Apaches and Wildcat reconnaissance helicopters and Royal Air Force Chinook support helicopters – took off for Finland and Estonia to train on Exercise Steadfast Defender 24. (APOSEC-OFFICIAL-20240424-013-0100.jpg)

An RAF Chinook (27(R) Squadron) flying in formation with a Puma (230 Squadron) over RAF Cosford in 2022. (CK-20220610-1006-COS JOIN-0019.jpg)

Apache, Merlin and Wildcat helicopters prepare to take part in a flypast for the 2023 King's Birthday Parade. (1AAC_OFFICIAL_Kings_Flypast0021.jpg)

A Reacher Large mobile X-Band satellite ground terminal (SGT) of 22nd Signal Regiment pictured in 2021. Staff at the Allied Rapid Reaction Corps deployed on exercise Steadfast Leda utilised these data links in order to communicate with the battlefield. Headquarters Allied Rapid Reaction Corps (HQ ARRC) provides NATO with a rapidly deployable, flexible HQ that can act as a Joint, Land or Corps HQ for operations and crisis response. The British lead HQ is based at Imjin Barracks in Gloucester. (45170278.jpg)

The last of the fixed-wing aircraft in use by the Army Air Corps (Islander and Defender) were transferred to the RAF in 2019 along with the personnel of 651 Squadron AAC; the aircraft were withdrawn from service in June 2021. The personnel returned to the AAC 1 August 2021 and the squadron reformed in 1st Regiment AAC. There were some fixed-wing trainer aircraft (Grob Tutor) in use by 674 Squadron AAC until it stood down in April 2021.

Allied Rapid Reaction Corps

The Allied Rapid Reaction Corps (ARRC) was created in October 1992, the first and then a model for what would be termed High Readiness Force (Land) HQs. It is a NATO and not a British Army HQ. Originally established at Bielefeld and built around the disbanded 1 (British) Corps HQ; the HQ moved to Rheindahlen in 1994 and to Imjin Barracks outside Gloucester in 2010. Forces are only assigned to the ARRC upon receipt of an activation order from the Supreme Allied Commander Europe (SACEUR). It commanded forces in Bosnia 1995–96 and Kosovo 1999. The corps later took command of the International Security Assistance Force (ISAF) in Afghanistan in 2006 and deployed there January 2011–January 2012. ARRC is always headed by a British lieutenant general. The chief of staff is also British, but the deputy commander and other positions can be from any of the NATO nations. The UK now provides about 80 percent of the funding and 60 percent of the staff for the corps. In 2017 there were personnel from 22 countries besides the UK in the ARRC HQ.

There are no combat formations permanently assigned to the ARRC. It was announced in 2021 that 1st (UK) Signal Brigade and 104th Logistic Support Brigade would both be resubordinated to ARRC. Before that, 1st (UK) Signal Brigade was under 6th (UK) Division and tasked for ARRC, while 104th Logistic Support Brigade was under 1st (UK) Division but similarly tasked for ARRC.

The ARRC Support Battalion became a Gurkha unit in 2021 and was redesignated that August. The ARRC Military Police Battalion is an AR unit; the reservists must be ex-military police, ex-police service, or have worked at the National Crime Agency. 30th Signal Regiment provides communications support to the Joint Rapid Reaction Force, Vanguard Aviation Force, Air Assault Task Force, Vanguard Field Hospital and Allied Rapid Reaction Force Headquarters. 250 (Gurkha) Signal Squadron supports the Commander Joint Forces Operations when deployed. The CO of 30 Signal Regiment is also the Commander of the Queen's Gurkha Signals.

1ST (UNITED KINGDOM) SIGNAL BRIGADE

HQ 1st (United Kingdom) Signal Brigade: Innsworth
13th Signal Regiment: Blandford Camp, Dorset [defensive cyber regiment, reformed 1 June 2020]
22nd Signal Regiment: Stafford [Provides Information Communications Services to the ARRC]
Gurkha ARRC Support Battalion: Innsworth
  Battalion HQ
  HQ Squadron [Signals and Catering Troops, QM Department, LAD REME]
  14 Squadron RLC [Close Support Troop (RGR and QGE), Power Troop (RE), Transport Troop (RLC and QOGLR), Forward Support Troop (RLC, QOGLR, QGE)]
ARRC Military Police Battalion [AR]: Winchester
30th Signal Regiment: Bramcote
32nd (Scottish) Signal Regiment [AR; RHQ Glasgow]
39th Signal Regiment (The Skinners) [AR; RHQ Bristol]
280 Signal Squadron: Blandford [part of NATO's 1st Signal Battalion; formerly 628 Signal Troop]
299th Signal Squadron [Special Communications] [AR; Bletchley]

104TH LOGISTIC SUPPORT BRIGADE

HQ 104th Logistic Support Brigade: South Cerney
17 Port and Maritime Regiment RLC: Marchwood
►Partnered with 165 (Wessex) Port and Enabling Regiment RLC [AR; RHQ Plymouth]
29 Postal Courier and Movement Regiment RLC: South Cerney
►Partnered with 162 Postal Courier and Movement Regiment RLC [AR; RHQ Nottingham]
9th Theatre Support Regiment RLC: Hullavington
►Partnered with 152nd (North Irish) Fuel Support Regiment RLC [AR; RHQ Belfast]
►Also partnered with 167 Catering Support Regiment RLC [AR; nationally recruited regiment]
2nd Operational Support Group RLC [AR]: Grantham
HQ Expeditionary Forces Institute and 148 EFI Squadron [AR]: Grantham
5th Force Support Battalion REME: Tidworth

152nd (North Irish) Fuel Support Regiment RLC [AR] was re-roled under *Army 2020* from a transport regiment to a fuel support regiment and subtitle changed to '(North Irish)'.
2nd Operational Support Group RLC [AR] provides staff officers and staff assistants to support operational HQs (497 Unit), specialist staff to employ and maintain local workforces abroad (498 Unit), specialist staff to ensure effective contracts abroad (499 Unit), and communications support to Army Medical Services (500 Troop).
104th Force Support Battalion REME [AR], formerly paired with 5th Force Support Battalion REME, was disbanded as part of the reduction of AR REME units in *Army 2020 Refine*.

3rd (UK) Division

3rd (UK) Division and its four assigned brigades were termed the Reaction Force under *Army 2020*. Both Reaction and Adaptable Force designations will disappear under *Future Soldier*. This was sometimes referred to as 3rd (UK) Mechanised Division although never officially designated as such and was regarded as available for service with the ARRC. According to its page on the British Army web site it 'is the only division at continual operational readiness in the UK.'

Under *Army 2020* the division had the 1st, 12th, and 20th Armoured Infantry and 101st Logistic Brigades. The first three were originally armoured brigades until reorganised and redesignated in January 2015. The 20th had been stationed in Germany with elements shifting to the UK; the last units returned in 2019. The combat brigades only had armoured and infantry units assigned to them. While each had dedicated artillery, engineer, and other support units, all of those units were under the command of 101st Logistic Brigade or Force Troops Command in peacetime.

In 2016, 25 (Close Support) Engineer Group HQ and three of its regiments (those supporting the three armoured infantry brigades) were transferred from 8 Engineer Brigade to 3rd (UK) Division. The group HQ had been HQ RE 3rd (UK) Division until *Army 2020*.

The three armoured infantry brigades were intended to operate on 36-month cycles, leaving one ready for contingent tasks. The first 12-month cycle was devoted to individual training, career courses and support of training. The next 12-month cycle was devoted to collective training. The final cycle had a brigade in readiness for operations for 12 months. One armoured task force in that brigade would have been at the highest readiness level. However, with *Army 2020 Refine* this system had to be abandoned.

The armoured infantry brigades were strong formations. Each had an armoured cavalry (formerly formation reconnaissance) regiment, an armoured regiment, two armoured infantry battalions, and a heavy protected mobility battalion. Each would have been supported on operations by an artillery regiment (AS90 SP 155mm gun and GMLRS batteries), an engineer regiment, a logistic support

A Challenger 2 Main Battle Tank, of 1 Royal Regiment of Fusiliers (1RRF) Battle Group, is shown returning to base after completing a firing mission as part of Exercise MedMan at the British Army Training Unit Suffield (BATUS) in Canada in 2005. (45148086.jpg)

A Warrior FV511 command vehicle at British Army Training Unit Suffield (BATUS). BATUS is located in Alberta, Canada and is one of the largest training areas the British Army use to exercise their armoured battle groups. It covers an area roughly seven times the size of the Salisbury Plain Training Area. (45148919.jpg)

A CVR(T) Scimitar from 1st Battalion, The Black Watch is pictured during a firepower demonstration on Salisbury Plain in 2005. (45149233.jpg)

Pictured is a British Army Royal Artillery GMLRS rocket launcher prepared to fire during Exercise Steel Sabre in 2016. The Guided Multiple Launch Rocket System (GMLRS), nicknamed the '70km Sniper', provides pinpoint accuracy delivering a 200lb high explosive warhead to its target, with twice the range of other artillery systems used by the British Army. (45159595.jpg)

regiment RLC, armoured close support battalion REME, and an armoured medical regiment. They could also gain the support of a signal regiment. However, none of those were under brigade control in peacetime. While some would come from 101st Logistic Brigade, others were from brigades in Force Troops Command. The first change to the division came in 2016, as noted, when the close support engineer group was transferred in. However, the regiments remained under the group – instead of the brigade they supported – in peacetime.

The division began major changes under *Army 2020 Refine*. The 12th and 20th Armoured Infantry Brigades were to remain, but in a much-reduced size: an armoured regiment and two armoured infantry battalions. Each of the latter would be paired with a light role Army Reserve battalion; previously all Army Reserve infantry battalions were paired with battalions in 1st (UK) Division. Note that these brigades no longer had any assigned recce units. The division would also have two strike brigades: the 1st and one whose brigade designation was not known. A strike brigade would have two armoured cavalry regiments and two mechanised – formerly heavy protected mobility – battalions. In theory one brigade of each type would be available for deployment in any 12-month period.

The reorganisation began with assembly of a strike experimentation group at Warminster and Catterick. 1st Armoured Infantry Brigade then began reorganising into 1st Strike Brigade. 101st Logistic Brigade remained assigned but would have some internal changes.

Elimination of Force Troops Command on 1 August 2019 – see 6th (UK) Division – resulted in the assignment of additional units to 3rd (UK) Division. It gained 1st Artillery Brigade, 7th Air Defence Group, and the three RMP regiments, quickly reduced to two. The three mixed artillery regiments formerly supporting the three armoured infantry brigades were reorganised into two regiments with the AS90 SP 155mm gun and a divisional deep fires regiment with the GMLRS. The SP regiments would support the two remaining armoured infantry brigades. The strike brigades – originally intended to have a 105mm Light Gun regiment for close support – were then to be left without any Regular artillery support when those regiments were scheduled to lose their guns. However, that decision was later reversed and the two regiments retained their 105mm Light Guns. 25 Engineer Group disbanded one of its existing armoured engineer regiments but regained two regiments formerly assigned to it but left with 8 Engineer Brigade. The two armoured engineer regiments would support the remaining armoured infantry brigades, and the other two regiments would support the new strike brigades.

On 16 October 2020 11th Signal Brigade transferred from 6th (UK) Division to 3rd (UK) Division, giving up its concurrent role as HQ West Midlands.

However, before the *Army 2020 Refine* changes could be fully implemented, the Army established a new force structure. The 12th and 20th Armoured Infantry Brigades would be reorganised as the 12th and 20th Armoured Brigade Combat Teams, each comprising an armoured cavalry regiment, an armoured regiment, and two mechanised infantry battalions in the new Boxer vehicles. In summer 2022 the 1st Artillery Brigade HQ would be disbanded, and its units would then be combined with the 1st Armoured Infantry (ex-Strike) Brigade to form the new 1st Deep Recce Strike Brigade Combat Team. 11th Signal Brigade would be reduced to 7th Signal Group, and 101st Logistic Brigade renamed as the 101st Operational Sustainment Brigade. The strike brigades would be abolished, with one temporarily resuming its former designation. The division would form a manoeuvre group with signals and military intelligence units.

In October 2022 the division oversaw the command post exercise Operation Cerberus 22 in Germany, based around the NATO Forward Holding Base Sennelager. This involved some 3,500 troops and 800 vehicles, including the following brigade HQs: 16th Air Assault Brigade Combat Team, 12th Armoured Brigade Combat Team, 7th Light Mechanised Brigade Combat Team, 101 Operational Sustainment Brigade, and 1st Aviation Brigade. ARRC provided overall NATO command and control over the exercise, with 3rd (UK) Division in actual command of the brigades. This was the first large-scale exercise in Europe since the Army left Germany and was intended to assess if each of the brigade HQs was ready for operations 'by testing their ability to plan and execute operations within a simulated warfighting scenario set in Europe' per an MOD news release. Some vehicles and equipment were moved from the UK and some were drawn from the stored vehicles and equipment at Sennelager. What is notable is that only one of the combat brigades was from 3rd (UK) Division itself.

For comparison, in 1984 the British Army undertook their largest ever exercise in Germany, Exercise Lionheart. That involved 131,500 troops (Regulars and reservists); over 60,000 of them moved by air and sea to Germany. That figure of 131,500 is, of course, larger than the entire British Army today, including the Army Reserve.

In a September 2023 speech, the CGS, General Sir Patrick Sanders, indicated that 3rd (UK) Division would be enhanced to warfight under the ARRC. In July 2024 the Army announced that 1st (UK) Division would be the Land Component Command of an all-new Allied Reaction Force (ARF). This is to be a multi-national force operating across the five domains of land, maritime, air, cyber and space. SACEUR will have at his disposal the 7th Light Mechanised Brigade Combat Team, aviation components, and an operational sustainment brigade supported by elements of 11th Security Force Assistance Brigade. The division will be under the command of the NATO Rapid Deployable Corps located near Milan, Italy.

This section largely shows the division as it was constituted prior to the Future Soldier changes, although it does discuss what those changes would be.

3RD (UK) DIVISION

3rd (UK) Division HQ and 3rd Divisional Signal Regiment: Bulford

12th Armoured Infantry Brigade

12th Armoured Infantry Brigade HQ and Signal Squadron (214): Bulford
Royal Tank Regiment [armour]: Tidworth
1st Bn The Royal Regiment of Fusiliers [armoured infantry]: Tidworth
►paired with 5th Bn The Royal Regiment of Fusiliers [light role infantry] [AR; HQ Newcastle upon Tyne]
1st Bn The Royal Welsh [armoured infantry]: Tidworth
►Paired with 3rd Bn The Royal Welsh [light role infantry] [AR; HQ Cardiff]
4th Armoured Close Support Battalion REME: Tidworth

In the change to two armoured infantry and two strike brigades, 12th Armoured Infantry Brigade gained the Royal Tank Regiment and 1st Bn Royal Regiment of Fusiliers from the former 1st Armoured Infantry Brigade and sent 1st Bn Yorkshire Regiment (converting from armoured infantry to mechanised) to 1st Strike Brigade, while the King's Royal Hussars and 1st Bn Scots Guards went to the Experimental Strike Group.

20TH ARMOURED INFANTRY BRIGADE

20th Armoured Infantry Brigade HQ and Signal Squadron (200): Bulford
Queen's Royal Hussars [armour]: Tidworth
1st Bn The Mercian Regiment [armoured infantry]: Bulford
►paired with 4th Bn The Mercian Regiment [light role infantry] [AR; HQ Wolverhampton]
5th Bn The Rifles [armoured infantry]: Bulford
►paired with 7th Bn The Rifles [light role infantry] [AR; HQ Kensington]
3rd Armoured Close Support Battalion REME: Tidworth
20th Armoured Infantry Brigade gained 1st Bn Mercian Regiment from the former 1st Armoured Infantry Brigade and sent to them The Royal Dragoon Guards.

1ST STRIKE [THEN ARMOURED INFANTRY] BRIGADE

1st Strike [Armoured Infantry] Brigade HQ and Signal Squadron (215): Tidworth
Royal Dragoon Guards [armoured cavalry]: Catterick
Royal Lancers (Queen Elizabeth's Own) [armoured cavalry]: Catterick
1st Bn The Yorkshire Regiment [mechanised infantry]: Catterick
3rd Bn The Rifles [mechanised infantry]: Catterick

1st Armoured Infantry Brigade converted to 1st Strike Brigade, and then resumed its former designation during 2021. It became HQ of the 1st Deep Recce Strike Brigade Combat Team with RAC and RA units 1 July 2022. The Royal Dragoon Guards came from 20th Armoured Infantry Brigade while 1st Bn Yorkshire Regiment came from 12th Armoured Infantry Brigade.

EXPERIMENTAL STRIKE GROUP

HQ Experimental Strike Group: Warminster
Household Cavalry Regiment [armoured cavalry]: Bulford
King's Royal Hussars [armoured cavalry]: Tidworth
1st Bn Scots Guards [mechanised infantry]: Aldershot
The Highlanders, 4th Bn Royal Regiment of Scotland [mechanised infantry]: Catterick

The Household Cavalry Regiment came from the 1st Armoured Infantry Brigade; the King's Royal Hussars was an armoured regiment in 12th Armoured Infantry Brigade and converted to armoured cavalry; 1st Bn Scots Guards also came from the 12th and The Highlanders from the 20th Armoured Infantry Brigade. The group would be broken up and its units reassigned under *Future Soldier*.

The Royal Wessex Yeomanry [AR: RHQ Bovington, Dorset] is paired with the two armour regiments with a role of providing fully trained tank crews and personnel. It was directly subordinated to 3rd (UK) Division.

1ST ARTILLERY BRIGADE

HQ 1st Artillery Brigade: Tidworth
1st Regiment RHA [AS90 SP 155mm gun]: Larkhill
3rd Regiment RHA [105mm Light Gun] [reorganised March 2023 as GMLRS]: Newcastle upon Tyne
4th Regiment RA: Topcliffe
19th Regiment RA: Larkhill
26th Regiment RA [GMLRS]: Larkhill
►paired with 101st (Northumbrian) Artillery Regiment [AR; RHQ Gateshead] [GMLRS]
103rd (Lancashire Artillery Volunteers) Regiment RA [AR; RHQ St Helens] [105mm Light Gun]
104th Regiment RA [AR; RHQ Newport, Wales] [105mm Light Gun]
105th Regiment RA [AR; RHQ Edinburgh] [105mm Light Gun]
Central Volunteer HQ RA: Woolwich
221st (Wessex) Battery RA [new: RA Specialist Pool]
255th (Somerset Yeomanry) Battery RA [tactical group]

1st Artillery Brigade transferred to the division 1 August 2019 from Force Troops Command, giving up its role as HQ South West which was separated; it had been under the operational command of the division since May 2018. Under *Future Soldier* it was disbanded 1 July 2022 and its units absorbed into the new 1st Deep Reconnaissance Strike Brigade Combat Team.

Soldiers of the Royal Artillery are pictured firing 105mm Light Guns during an exercise in 2013. (45155621.jpg)

1st Regiment RHA and 19th Regiment RA re-roled under *Army 2020* as all-gun units, trading batteries with 26th Regiment RA. In turn, it became an all-GMLRS regiment.

3rd Regiment RHA re-roled summer 2023 with the GMLRS and Exactor and reorganised.

101st (Northumbrian Artillery) Regiment RA re-roled from 105mm Light Gun to GMLRS under *Army 2020.*

104th Regiment RA transferred to the brigade 2017 and converted to a light gun regiment. It had been in 1st ISTAR Brigade as a UAS [drone] regiment.

7TH AIR DEFENCE GROUP

HQ 7th Air Defence Group: Thorney Island
12th Regiment RA [Strarstreak HVM]: Thorney Island
►paired with 106th (Yeomanry) Regiment RA [AR; RHQ Grove Park, London] [Stormer and LML]
16th Regiment RA [Sky Sabre]: Thorney Island

7th Air Defence Group was formed by redesignation of Joint Ground Based Air Defence Headquarters 1 April 2019 when the air defence regiments were placed under 3rd (UK) Division. HQ had been at High Wycombe. The group was initially under the administrative control of 1st Artillery Brigade. The Royal Artillery assumed sole responsibility for ground-based air defence back in 2004.

12th Regiment RA currently has three SP HVM (Stormer) batteries (one for each of the prior armoured infantry brigades) and one LML battery, tasked to support 16th Air Assault Brigade. It was supposed to convert one SP battery to LML and add another LML battery (to support the two strike brigades). It now has four SP batteries and one LML battery.

16th Regiment RA converted beginning in 2020 from Rapier FSC to the new Sky Sabre SAM; this was completed in 2022.

Shown here is an HVM Stormer from 9 Battery, 12 Regiment RA, searching for enemy aircraft over the hills of the Sauerland, Germany during the multi-national Exercise Falcon Force. (45109434.jpg)

25 (CLOSE SUPPORT) ENGINEER GROUP

HQ 25 (CS) Engineer Group: Minley
21 Engineer Regiment: Ripon [field CS]
22 Engineer Regiment: Perham Down [armoured CS]; tasked to support 20th Armoured Infantry Brigade
26 Engineer Regiment: Perham Down [armoured CS]; tasked to support 12th Armoured Infantry Brigade
32 Engineer Regiment: Catterick [field CS]
Royal Monmouthshire RE (Militia) [AR; RHQ Monmouth Castle] [field CS]]

25 (Close Support) Engineer Group was organised 1 August 2014 by redesignation and reorganisation of 3rd Division Engineer Group and placed under 8 Engineer Brigade. It originally had three regiments tasked to support the 1st, 12th and 20th Armoured Infantry Brigades and two regiments tasked to support the Adaptable Force. When the group was transferred to 3rd (UK) Division in 2016 it brought only the three regiments supporting the armoured infantry brigades. Under *Army 2020 Refine* 35 Engineer Regiment in Germany was to be re-roled as EOD and Search on return to the UK, and 21 and 32 Engineer Regiments were reorganised and rejoined the group. Two squadrons from 35 Engineer Regiment were transferred to 21 and 32 Regiments and reorganised from armoured to field to give them three Regular field squadrons each; they then released their AR squadrons.

Pictured is a Trojan Armoured Engineering Vehicle in Sennelager, Germany during Exercise Tallinn Dawn in 2022. Trojan is an armoured engineer vehicle designed to open routes through complex battlefield obstacles and clear a path through minefields. (45169726.jpg)

101ST LOGISTIC BRIGADE

HQ 101st Logistic Brigade and Signal Troop (661): Aldershot
1 Close Support Logistics Regiment RLC: Graven Hill, Bicester
►Partnered with 157 (Welsh) Transport Regiment RLC [AR; RHQ Cardiff]
3 Close Support Logistics Regiment RLC: Abingdon
►Partnered with 151 Transport Regiment RLC [AR; RHQ Croydon]
4 Close Support Logistics Regiment RLC: Abingdon
►Partnered with 154 (Scottish) Transport Regiment RLC [AR; RHQ Dunfermline]
10 The Queen's Own Gurkha Logistics Regiment [Force Support]: Aldershot
27 Regiment RLC [Force Support]: Aldershot
156 Supply Regiment RLC [AR; RHQ Liverpool]
6th Armoured Close Support Battalion REME: Tidworth
102nd (Force Support) Battalion REME [AR; HQ Newton Aycliff]
103rd (Force Support) Battalion REME [AR; HQ Crawley]
1st Regiment RMP [RHQ Catterick]
3rd Regiment RMP [RHQ Bulford]

The brigade's RLC and REME elements were reorganised under *Army 2020 Refine*. The three RMP regiments were transferred in from 1st Military Police Brigade in 2019, and then reduced to two. The armoured medical regiments formerly assigned went to 2nd Medical Brigade in 1st (UK) Division at the same time. The AR 102nd and 106th Battalions REME were merged and reorganised, as were the 103rd and 104th Battalions. This was part of the reduction in AR REME units.

81mm training rounds being moved into the Queens Own Gurkha Logistic Regiment Ammo Stores on Ex Steadfast Defender, Drawsko Pomorskie Training Area (DPTA), Poland in February 2024. (AHQCPL4-OFFICIAL-20240229-018-028.jpg)

11TH SIGNAL BRIGADE

HQ 11th Signal Brigade: Donnington, Shropshire
  10th Signal Regiment [RHQ: Corsham]
7th Signal Group
  HQ 7th Signal Group: Donnington, to move to Bulford
  1st Signal Regiment: Stafford, to move to Perham Down
  15th Signal Regiment: Blandford
  16th Signal Regiment: Stafford
  21st Signal Regiment: Colerne
  32nd Signal Regiment [AR; RHQ Glasgow]
  37th Signal Regiment [AR; RHQ Redditch]

HQ South Midlands separated from HQ 11th Signal Brigade when the brigade transferred to 3rd (UK) Division. 2nd Signal Group, formed under *Army 2020* from the former 2nd Signal Brigade, was later disbanded and its units placed directly under the brigade or reassigned.

10th Signal Regiment provides a variety of specialised services; see details in the section on Royal Corps of Signals.

7th Signal Group supported 3rd (UK) Division, the Reaction Force.
1st Signal Regiment supported 20th Armoured Infantry Brigade
16th Signal Regiment supported the 12th Armoured Infantry Brigade.
21st Signal Regiment supported the 1st Armoured Infantry Brigade, remaining with it as 1st Strike Brigade and then when it resumed its former designation. It will be converted to an electronic warfare and signals intelligence unit and reassigned.

A female Royal Signals soldier readies a Falcon vehicle during Exercise Flying Falcon 16 (Ex FF16). Ex Flying Falcon 16 (Ex FF16) was an 11 Signal & West Midland Brigade field exercise run to ensure the competence in the provision of a fully integrated and managed network to enable Command and Control. Falcon is a fully deployable, tactical military communications system that provides users the capability to interface seamlessly with a wide range of other systems. This capability means that voice, data and video information can be shared securely across all elements of the battlespace through the use of one common platform. (45170288.jpg)

16th Air Assault Brigade Combat Team

As noted earlier, until November 2015 this brigade was under the control of Joint Helicopter Command. In that month it was transferred (less the AAC regiments and its REME battalion) to the direct command of HQ Field Army. It forms the Army element of the Rapid Reaction Force and maintains one battlegroup (termed the Air Assault Task Force) at high readiness for deployment anywhere in the world.

The original plan under *Army 2020* was to reduce the brigade to the two parachute battalions, and the artillery and engineer regiments each gave up an operational battery or squadron. Later, the UK-based Gurkha battalion was assigned to the brigade. In August 2021 1st Bn The Royal Irish Regiment rejoined the brigade, which would become 16th Air Assault Brigade Combat Team. All units are at Colchester, Essex, unless otherwise indicated. At least until full implementation of *Future Soldier*, the two infantry battalions remain under the administrative control of 11th Infantry Brigade. At that point they will be supported by the new RPOC.

In a September 2023 speech, the CGS, General Sir Patrick Sanders, indicated that the brigade would be brought under 1st (UK) Division in 2024.

Soldiers from the 3rd Battalion, Parachute Regiment, are seen here before boarding a Puma helicopter for fast roping serials in 2012. (45168137.jpg)

16TH AIR ASSAULT BRIGADE COMBAT TEAM

16th Air Assault Brigade HQ and Air Assault Signal Squadron (216)
2nd Bn The Parachute Regiment
3rd Bn The Parachute Regiment
1st Bn The Royal Irish Regiment: Tern Hill [light recce strike infantry]
1st Bn The Royal Gurkha Rifles: Shorncliffe [air assault infantry]: replaced June-July 2022 by 2nd Bn
2nd Bn The Royal Gurkha Rifles: Folkstone [air assault infantry]
Pathfinder Platoon
7th Parachute Regiment RHA [105mm Light Gun]
A (1st City of London) Battery, Honourable Artillery Company [AR] [105mm Light Gun]
23 Parachute Engineer Regiment: Woodbridge (Suffolk)
13 Air Assault Support Regiment RLC
16 Medical Regiment

4th Bn The Parachute Regiment [AR; HQ Pudsey, Leeds] is paired with the two battalions in 16th Air Assault Brigade. The brigade would be supported on operations by 12 (Minden) Air Assault Battery RA [Starstreak HVM] from 12 Regiment RA at Thorney Island, 21 (Gibraltar 1779-83) Air Assault Battery RA [UAS] from 47 Regiment RA at Larkhill, and 53 (Louisburg) Battery RA [STA] from 5 Regiment RA at Catterick. It is also supported by 156 Provost Company (Air Assault) from 3rd Regiment RMP, co-located at Colchester. It is no longer supported by D Squadron, Household Cavalry Regiment.
The 1st and 2nd Bns Royal Gurkha Rifles rotate between Brunei and the UK every three years.

7th Parachute Regiment RHA was reduced from three to two gun-batteries when the brigade was cut to two battalions under *Army 2020*. Another battery reformed in 2023 as a gun battery. In 2023 it also received a tactical group battery from 3rd RHA. The Honourable Artillery Company battery provides two guns and crews to each Regular 105mm battery.

1st Royal Irish, in their light recce strike role, are mounted in Jackal and Foxhound patrol vehicles. Their CO referred to them in a May 2023 interview as 'a semi-mechanised battalion.... We give the Brigade Commander eyes and ears over the horizon.' Prior to *Army 2020* the battalion had long served as the brigade's air assault infantry battalion.

Soldiers from 7 Parachute Regiment Royal Horse Artillery (7 RHA), as part of the 3rd Battalion The Parachute Regiment Battlegroup, fire live rounds with their 105mm Light Gun during Ex Askari Storm Kenya in 2020. (45166110.jpg)

Soldiers from the 3rd Battalion the Parachute Regiment about to undertake a compound clearance on a Combined Arms Live Fire Exercise in Kenya during Ex Askari Storm in the British Army's Nanyuki Training Area, Kenya. (45166115.jpg)

1st (UK) Division

1st (UK) Division was the Adaptable Force under *Army 2020*. At one time, on its official web page, the division described itself as heading up 'the British Army's Light Role Adaptable Force'. They went on to say that the division 'is configured to deliver "light role excellence"'. Now it describes itself as 'the British Army's most versatile force – light, agile, lethal and expeditionary. Active and effective at home and overseas. Trusted by defence and the nation as a multi-talented workforce with unique capabilities.' As noted, the terms Reaction Force and Adaptable Force will disappear under *Future Soldier*.

The division began with a large number of infantry brigades, each of which also served as a regional headquarters. In their territorial role as the regional point of command (RPOC), they provided support to all Regular and Army Reserve units based within their area of responsibility. 1st (UK) Division had almost all of these, although two brigades in Force Troops Command also had an RPOC role. Neither 1st (UK) Division nor any of its brigades was deployable, although in theory it once had 'a light brigade at readiness for operations at all times' from its web page in 2019. Formerly 1st (UK) Armoured Division in Germany, division HQ was redesignated 1st (UK) Division and relocated to York in 2015. In addition to the infantry brigades, the division had 102nd Logistic Brigade, which also moved its headquarters from Germany.

When it was formed, 1st (UK) Division had 4th Infantry Brigade and HQ North East (Catterick), 7th Infantry Brigade and HQ East (Chilwell), 11th Infantry Brigade and HQ South East (Aldershot), 38th (Irish) Brigade (Lisburn), 42nd Infantry Brigade and HQ North West (Preston), 51st Infantry Brigade and HQ Scotland (moved from Stirling to Edinburgh in 2018), and 160th Infantry Brigade and HQ Wales (Brecon). 42nd Infantry Brigade was disbanded in 2017 and a distinct HQ North West established in its place; in effect this was simply a redesignation. A Specialised Infantry Group was established at Aldershot in October 2017 to control infantry battalions assuming that new role.

A number of changes were made under *Army 2020 Refine* July–August 2019. The number of infantry brigades was reduced to four, with armour and infantry consolidated among them. 102nd Logistic Brigade HQ was marked for disbanding with its units to be reorganised and reassigned. However this was later put on hold and ultimately abandoned. The Specialised Infantry Group was transferred to the new 6th (UK) Division, formed out of part of the former Force Troops Command. 1st (UK) Division also gained control of 8 Engineer Brigade, 2nd Medical Brigade, and 104th Logistic Support Brigade from Force Troops Command.

In August 2021 the 11th Infantry Brigade became 11th Security Force Assistance Brigade. The brigade would assume the role previously held by the Specialised Infantry Group, which was redesignated August 2021 as the Army Special Operations Brigade. The 104th Logistic Support Brigade has been resubordinated to the Allied Rapid Reaction Corps.

Under *Future Soldier*, this will become an operational division with deployable elements. 4th Infantry Brigade will become the 4th Light Brigade Combat Team; 7th Infantry Brigade will become the 7th Light Mechanised Brigade Combat Team; 11th will retain its designation and role as a security force assistance brigade; and 51st Brigade and HQ Scotland will transfer to Regional Command. The 4th, 7th and 11th Brigades will all give up their role as area RPOCs and the area HQs will also transfer to Regional Command. 19th Brigade would reform at York, taking over responsibility for a number of Army Reserve units; it reformed there 23 July 2022. 102nd Logistic Brigade will become 102nd Operational Sustainment Brigade. The division will form a manoeuvre group with signals and military intelligence units.

In a September 2023 speech, the CGS, General Sir Patrick Sanders, indicated that 16th Air Assault Brigade Combat Team would come under 1st (UK) Division in 2024, with the division 'becoming a land component command of a joint and multi-domain sovereign Global Response Force (GRF) by 2024, as "an agile tool of foreign policy able to deliver rapid global effects and be first to the fight. This is a return to fielding a second battle-winning division HQ."'

This section shows the division as it was constituted prior to the *Future Soldier* changes.

1ST (UK) DIVISION

HQ 1st (UK) Division: York
2nd Signal Regiment: York, to move to Catterick

4th Infantry Brigade and Headquarters North East
HQ 4th Infantry Brigade and Headquarters North East: Catterick
The Light Dragoons [light role cavalry: Catterick
►Partnered with The Queen's Own Yeomanry [light role cavalry] [AR: RHQ Newcastle upon Tyne]
2nd Bn The [Royal] Yorkshire Regiment [light role infantry]: Catterick
►Partnered with 4th Bn The [Royal] Yorkshire Regiment [light role infantry] [AR; HQ York]
1st Battalion Duke of Lancaster's Regiment [light role infantry]: Chester
►Partnered with 4th Bn The Duke of Lancaster's Regiment [light role infantry] [AR; HQ Preston]
2nd Bn The Mercian Regiment [light role infantry]: Weeton Barracks
►Partnered with 4th Bn The Mercian Regiment [light role infantry] [AR; HQ Wolverhampton]
Royal Highland Fusiliers, 2nd Bn The Royal Regiment of Scotland [light role infantry]: Peniculk
►Partnered with 52nd Lowland Volunteers, 6th Bn The Royal Regiment of Scotland [light role infantry] [AR; HQ Glasgow]

This will become the 4th Light Brigade Combat Team under *Future Soldier* and the HQ North East will be separated.
The Yorkshire Regiment became The Royal Yorkshire Regiment 6 April 2023.
The Royal Highland Fusiliers (2 Scots) transferred from 51st Infantry Brigade 1 August 2019, as did the 52nd Lowland Volunteers (6 Scots).

This photo shows a Light Dragoon Jackal 2 patrol vehicle in action as part of Operation Newcombe, in support of United Nations Multidimensional Integrated Stabilization Mission in Mali (MINUSMA), in 2021. (45168171.jpg)

7TH INFANTRY BRIGADE AND HEADQUARTERS EAST

HQ 7th Infantry Brigade and Headquarters East: Cottesmore
1st The Queen's Dragoon Guards [light role cavalry]: Swanton Morley
►Partnered with The Royal Yeomanry [light role cavalry: [AR: RHQ Leicester 2021]
1st Bn The Royal Anglian Regiment [light role infantry]: Woolwich: Deployed to Dhekelia, Cyprus July 2021
2nd Bn The Royal Anglian Regiment [light role infantry]: Cottesmore
►Partnered with 3rd Bn The Royal Anglian Regiment [light role infantry] [AR; HQ Bury St Edmonds]
4th Bn The Princess of Wales's Royal Regiment [light role infantry] [AR; HQ Redhill]
1st Bn The Rifles [light role infantry]: Chepstow
►Partnered with 6th Bn The Rifles [light role infantry] [AR; HQ Exeter]

7th Infantry Brigade will become 7th Light Mechanised Brigade Combat Team; HQ East will be separated and transferred.
4th Bn The Princess of Wales's Royal Regiment is partnered with 1st Bn of regiment when the Regular battalion is in the UK.
1st Bn and 6th Bn The Rifles transferred from 160th Infantry Brigade 1 August 2019.

The Royal Anglian Regiment (using Foxhound vehicles) conduct a dawn attack for the Media Day, during Ex Steadfast Defender, Drawsko Pomorskie Training Area (DPTA), Poland, on the morning of 26 February 2024. (AHQCPL4-OFFICIAL-20240226-015-041.jpg)

The origins of the Challenger 2 MBT lie in the Vickers Defence Systems Mk 7 design, worked up into the Challenger 2 in close consultation with the MOD in the late 1980s. Much of the design was constrained by questions of cost and the speed with which a new tank could be brought into service. Many pages could be written on the selection process and competition but it suffices here to say that Challenger 2 was selected over several foreign designs, including the M1A1 Abrams and Leopard 2. The final choice used what was essentially a product improved Challenger hull and engine with a new turret mounting the British L30 120mm rifled gun. The armour was an improved version of the earlier Chobham referred to as Dorchester Level 1 but designed from the outset to accept additional Operational Armour Packs when deployed on operations. The first operational deployment was to Kosovo in 2000 on Op Agricola 3, followed by Iraq in 2003 under Op Telic. The example shown here has been upgraded to Theatre Entry Standard (TES) and has additional armour on the glacis 'toe', and to protect the sides of the hull and turret. In addition, 'bar' armour has been applied around the engine compartment and turret rear to provide additional protection versus weapons such as RPGs. (Artwork by David Bocquelet)

Shown here is the much-photographed Challenger 2, from the Armoured Trials & Development Unit (ATDU) based at Bovington, known as Megatron. This example has been used to demonstrate and trial a wide range of incremental improvements including a remote weapon station above the commander's cupola that enables the 7.62mm GPMG to be fired under-armour. The upper rear of the turret mounts a number of antennas for communications and electronic countermeasures systems. Megatron retains the L30 120mm rifled gun and this single feature has essentially rendered the Challenger 2 near obsolete in peer-versus-peer tank combat: being a rifled weapon the L30 is unable to achieve muzzle velocities as great as the rival 120mm Rhinemetall (or US derivative), or Soviet/Russian 125mm gun designs. Furthermore, where the L30 uses separate projectiles and charges, the Rhinemetall gun uses single-piece ammunition and the two are not compatible; the British gun is therefore unable to use the latest long-rod penetrators or other advanced ammunition natures shared by NATO and other allies. A final complication is that whilst a straight replacement of the L30 with the Rhinemetall gun would be relatively easy to accomplish, the internal dimensions of the Challenger 2 turret mean it cannot accommodate more than a very small handful of rounds of single-piece 120mm ammunition. The ultimate solution is therefore a new turret mounting the Rhinemetall gun, along with a new electronic architecture, to be incorporated into the Challenger 3 design (see Volume 2). (Artwork by David Bocquelet).

The Scimitar had a long career with the British Army as part of the Combat Vehicle Reconnaissance (Tracked) (CVRT) family that included such vehicles as the Scorpion, Spartan and Sultan, amongst others. Originally introduced to British Army service in the mid-1970s, the Scimitar served in the Close Recce and Formation Recce roles until finally withdrawn from service only in April 2023, despite being described as dangerously obsolete and in urgent need of replacement even in the late 1980s. The Scimitar is armed with the L21A1 30mm Rarden cannon and whilst theoretically capable of fully automatic fire this was greatly restricted by the fact that the weapon fired from three-round clips manually loaded into the breach; nevertheless, this was considered an accurate weapon and was popular with crews. The CVRT family was slated for replacement by the ASCOD-derived Ajax family but this programme has been as much delayed and much troubled and at the time of writing the Ajax has still not entered operational service. As an interim measure the FV510 Warrior is being used in some cavalry roles pending the arrival of Ajax. (Artwork by David Bocquelet)

The FV510 Warrior family of vehicles first entered service with the British Army in 1988 and provided mobility for the infantry to keep pace with the Challenger MBT, with most variants carrying the L21A1 Rarden 30mm gun. Originally known as the MCV-80 (Mechanised Combat Vehicle for the 80s), this vehicle was designed and built by GKN Sankey in the UK and was intended to be the base vehicle for a wide range of sub-variants including a mortar carrier and dedicated ATGW carrier; few of these ever came to fruition and the wider family was ultimately restricted to a few 'lookalike' command or AOP versions and an ARV, though the Bowman communications system and a thermal sight were introduced in an upgrade programme. A Warrior Capability Sustainment Programme was planned and would have included the 40mm CTA gun mounted in a new turret, however this programme was cancelled in 2021 when it was announced that Warrior would be retired and replaced by Boxer around the middle of the 2020s. Warrior appears to have found a new, albeit temporary, lease of life as a short-term substitute for Ajax in cavalry formations. The example shown here is in its basic configuration and without any additional armour packages as would usually be installed for operational deployments. (Artwork by David Bocquelet)

The FV432 is a classic 'battle taxi' design that first entered service with the British Army in the early 1960s and is analogous to the US M113 design. The Mk 2 entered service from 1965 and is identifiable by the exhaust system mounted on the left side of the hull. An upgraded and re-engined Mk 3 (often referred to as the Bulldog) entered service in 2006 as a relatively lightweight MICV for use in Iraq: this version could be fitted with a variety of additional armour packages and ECM equipment to defeat roadside IEDs. The basic 'box on tracks' design has continued to serve alongside the Warrior in Armoured Infantry battalions fulfilling many of the support roles that did not require the more complex vehicle's design. With the Warrior being retired from service imminently it seems likely that the FV430 family will share a similar fate, with both types being replaced by Boxer. (Artwork by David Bocquelet)

The Mastiff PPV (Protected Patrol Vehicle) is a British 6x6 variant of the Cougar MRAP family originally built by Force Protection Inc. and first used by the USMC. Introduced to service with British forces in December 2006, the Mastiff provided urgently needed protection against IEDs through use of a V-shaped monocoque hull. The Mk 2, introduced in 2009, allowed for crew of two and eight passengers. Provision for a range of roof-mounted weapons such as the 7.62mm GPMG, .50-cal Browning HMG, or a 40mm grenade machine gun, is included in the design. This example has improved side armour covering the passenger vision ports in the hull-side seen in early models, along with extensive bar armour to provide stand-off protection against high-explosive anti-tank weapons (as employed by RPGs for example), and a simple but effective wire-cutter mounted above the driver's compartment. A number of sub-variants exist, including the Wolfhound Tactical Support Vehicle with an open cargo bed, an example of which was used to carry the Laser Directed Energy Weapon tested in summer 2024. (Artwork by David Bocquelet)

Experience in Afghanistan during Op Herrick demonstrated the vulnerability of the CVRT family, including the Scimitar, to IEDs. BAE Systems undertook Project Transformer to manufacture around 60 members of the CVRT family to the Mk 2 standard, including some 30 Scimitars. The Scimitar Mk 2 essentially mated the Spartan hull with the Scimitar turret. The greater internal volume allowed for much improved crew seating and other measures to provide additional protection against mines. Protection against ballistic threats was also improved through the use of bar armour, and an extensive ECM suite was fitted. Some examples included the Roll-Over Protection System (not shown here), a heavy framework of tubes around the turret roof to protect exposed crew in the event of the vehicle being flipped over. The Scimitar Mk 2 remained in service post-Afghanistan and examples were deployed on Op Cabrit to Latvia in 2020. (Artwork by David Boquelet)

The Ajax programme was originally part of the Future Rapid Effects System (FRES) intended to deliver a Scout Vehicle (SV) and Utility Vehicle (UV). The General Dynamics Ajax was selected to provide the SV in 2016. Based on the existing ASCOD design already in service with Austria and Spain, this should in theory have been a relatively simple procurement programme. However, as has been played out very publicly, the programme has been fraught with manufacturing difficulties, late deliveries, vibration and hearing injuries to service personnel involved in the test programme and public statements by officials that these issues may never be fully resolved. From 2023 however, public reporting began to indicate a very sudden and dramatic improvement in the situation; whether this results in successful deliveries and a usable family of vehicles remains to be seen. Shown here is an early Ajax model fitted with the 40mm CTA cannon, one of what should become a family of vehicles with a similar breadth of scope to the CVRT family. (Artwork by David Bocquelet)

The other component of the FRES programme was the Utility Vehicle (UV). A number of designs competed for this, including the Boxer, in which the UK had been a partner between 1996 and 2003. Germany, the Netherlands, Lithuania and Australia have all successfully introduced the Boxer to service with deliveries ongoing. In 2019 the UK announced that it would rejoin the programme and with an option to order over 600 vehicles would potentially become one of the largest operators of the type. With a wide number of different variants included in the British order, the Boxer appears likely to replace both the Warrior and FV430 families in their current roles. The example shown here was unveiled by Rhinemetall to announce the British selection of Boxer in 2019. (Artwork by David Bocquelet).

The AS-90 (Artillery System for the 90s) built by VSEL was introduced to British service in 1993 to replace the aging M109 variants, Abbot 105mm SP gun and the towed 155mm FH-70. It is armed with a NATO-compatible 39-calibre 155mm howitzer able to fire all standard ammunition natures (plans to upgrade this to a 52-calibre weapon did not come to fruition). The AS-90 has seen active service in the Balkans and in Iraq. Whilst 57 AS-90s remained in service in 2023, at least 36 examples have been donated to Ukraine, where they have seen active service and a number have been lost in action. Swedish-built Archer wheeled artillery systems have been received by the British Army as an interim replacement pending delivery of the Boxer-based RCH-155 system. (Artwork by David Bocquelet)

The standard rocket artillery system of the British Army is the Guided Multiple Launch Rocket System (GMLRS), the A2 derivative of the M270 MRLS system. Originally designed to deliver cluster munitions and scatterable mines (now withdrawn under the terms of the 1997 Ottawa Convention), the current version uses the M31 munition with a 200lb unitary warhead delivered by GPS-guided rockets to ranges in excess of 70km. The GMLRS is being upgraded under the 2021 Land Deep Fires Programme and is intended to equip two Regular regiments and one Reserve regiment. (Artwork by David Bocquelet)

It was announced in April 2024 that Britain had selected the RCH-155 (Remote Controlled Howitzer 155mm), mounted on the Boxer chassis, as a replacement for the AS-90. It is planned that 116 vehicles, built jointly in the UK and Germany, will be delivered before the end of the 2020s. The RCH-155 is an example of the ability of the Boxer chassis to accept a wide variety of modules with different mission packages. The turret, armed with a NATO-compatible 155mm 52-calibre howitzer, can hold 30 rounds of ammunition, plus the necessary propellant charges, and is operated remotely, thus reducing crew exposure to counter-fire and other hazardous conditions such as a contaminated environment. Furthermore, the vehicle is capable of rapid emplacement and displacement, thus reducing the ability of an enemy to locate and target its firing position. (Artwork by David Bocquelet)

The BvS10 Viking is used by the Armoured Support Group of the Royal Marines in variants that include a troop carrier, a command carrier, a recovery and repair vehicle and an ambulance. In addition to a weapon station above the forward compartment, an L16 81mm mortar can be carried and fired from the rear compartment. The Viking is designed to minimise ground pressure in order to enable movement over snow, a feature that also proved useful in the often-difficult terrain of Helmand, even though radically different from the originally envisaged operating environment. The BvS10 was fitted with additional bar armour when used in Helmand. (Artwork by David Bocquelet)

The Jackal was originally developed for use by the British Army and Royal Marines in Afghanistan. Also known as the MWMIK (Mobility Weapon Mount Installation Kit), this vehicle is based on the Supercat HMT 400. The original Jackal entered service in 2008, followed in 2008–09 by the Jackal 2, that included a range of minor improvements such as a repositioned upper gun ring enabling a better field of fire. Intended as a vehicle for patrols and deep reconnaissance, the Jackal has only limited protection against direct and indirect fires due to its open structure, though various panels are reinforced with ballistic material and the vehicle offers a high level of mine resistance, unobstructed fields of visibility for the crew have been prioritised. The Jackal can be fitted with a variety of weapons including the 7.62mm GPMG, .50-cal HMG and the 40mm GMG, and other weapons can be carried by the crew, including for example, the man-portable Javelin ATGW. The Jackal has remained in widespread service with the British Army in a cavalry and reconnaissance role. The Coyote, a version with an extended rear bed, intended as a supply and support vehicle, is also in service. (Artwork by David Bocquelet)

The main provider of logistics vehicles to the British Army is now RMMV (Rhinemetall MAN Military Vehicles). Awarded a contract in 2005, the British armed forces use nearly 7,500 support vehicles, plus trailers, supplied by RMMV, primarily from the HX and SX model ranges to replace the older Bedford, Foden and DAF models. Shown here is a basic flatbed configuration of the HX77 version, though the chassis can be fitted with a wide range of body types for specialist roles, including bulk fuel tankers, and is also used to carry the Sky Sabre SAM system (see Volume 2). Other variants include cabs with ballistic protection and bar armour. A weapon such as the GPMG can also be fitted above the cab. (Artwork by David Bocquelet)

The Lynx AH.7 was used by both the Army Air Corps and the Royal Marines armed with TOW anti-tank missiles, or configured as a light battlefield helicopter (LBH) unarmed – as seen here – or fitted with a pintle-mounted 7.62mm GPMG, carrying up to nine passengers. Though fast, versatile, popular and reliable, the Lynx lacked any armoured protection and was replaced in the anti-tank and attack role by the Apache AH.1 in the 2000s. The AH.7, and later AH.9, models were fully replaced by the Wildcat by 2018. (Artwork by Rolando Ungolini)

Various models of the Boeing CH-47 Chinook have formed the backbone of the Royal Air Force's Support Helicopter fleet since 1980 and have regularly been deployed in support of Army operations. The model shown here is an HC2, and these began undergoing the Project Julius upgrade programme to HC4 standard around 2008, with initial operating capability achieved in 2012 and deliveries continuing well into the later 2010s. In their turn, the HC4s have now been replaced by the HC5, HC6 and HC6A standards, though all retain a similar and distinctive external appearance. (Artwork by Rolando Ungolini)

The other commonly seen RAF support helicopter is the Puma. Originally the French SA330 design, Pumas for RAF use were manufactured in the UK by Westland. First entering service in the early 1970s, and capable of carrying between 12 and 16 troops or two tonnes of cargo internally or as an underslung load, the Puma has seen very extensive use in support of Britian's armed forces ever since. The type is now reaching the end of its service life with the RAF and with just a dozen or so still in service is likely to be fully retired in the very near future. The RAF did adopt the Merlin in a similar role but all examples have now been passed to the Royal Navy. (Artwork by Rolando Ungolini)

General Sir Roly Walker KCB DSO was commissioned into the Irish Guards in 1993 and is the current Chief of the General Staff (CGS), the professional head of the Army. In this role he reports to the Chief of the Defence Staff (CDS) and, as a Service COS, has a right of direct access to the Secretary of State and the Prime Minister. He is shown here wearing the British Army's current MTP (multi-terrain pattern) uniform introduced in 2010 to replace several previous patterns including DPM (disruptive pattern material) and is based on a system developed by Crye Precision in the US. His rank insignia, running from top to bottom, shows a crown above a star, with a crossed sword and baton, all above the royal cypher of King Charles III. On his right shoulder he wears parachute wings. (Artwork by Renato Delmaso)

Perhaps one of the most iconic ceremonial uniforms of the British Army is that of the Household Cavalry Mounted Regiment (HCMR). The HCMR consists of elements of The Life Guards (shown here) and The Blues and Royals. The Life Guards are the senior regiment of the British Army and in addition to their ceremonial role also have an operational role as an Armoured Cavalry regiment based at Bulford. The trooper shown here wears a red tunic and a polished metal cuirass; the Albert Helmet was introduced in 1843 and The Life Guards wear it with a white plume and with the chin strap below the lower lip. The other component of the HCMR are the Blues and Royals, distinguished by their blue tunics, red plume, and the helmet strap worn under the chin. (Artwork by Renato Delmaso)

Another iconic image of the British Army's ceremonial appearance is presented by this sergeant of the Grenadier Guards. The five regiments of the Foot Guards are, in order of precedence the Grenadier Guards, Coldstream Guards, Scots Guards, Irish Guards and the Welsh Guards. Each regiment has a similar overall appearance, wearing a red tunic and a tall bearskin cap, with distinctions in the arrangement of the tunic buttons and hackle (the small plume worn on the side of the bearskin, not visible in this artwork, in white for the Grenadier Guards) in addition to more obvious regimental collar insignia such as the flaming grenade of the Grenadier Guards. This sergeant's rank is indicated by the gold chevrons worn on the right sleeve and the sash worn from the right shoulder. He carries the SA-80 rifle with black covers fastened over the plastic furniture and sight unit. The regiments of the Foot Guards all have an operational role as light role infantry or security force assistance battalions, other than the Scots Guards who fulfil the mechanised infantry role. (Artwork by Renato Delmaso)

All remaining Scottish line infantry regiments were merged to form the Royal Regiment of Scotland in 2006, sharing a No.1 Dress combining traditions from all of the antecedent regiments. Head dress consists of the Lowland pattern Glengarry with blackcock feathers and a red and white band. The cap badge consists of a saltire with lion rampant and the motto is Nemo Me Impune Lacessit (No One Assails Me With Impunity). Other traditions carried forwards include (but are not limited to) a uniform consisting of a doublet and a kilt in a version of the Government (Black Watch) tartan, hose and garter flashes also from the Black Watch, and spats and brogues from the Gordon Highlanders. The Tam O'Shanter worn at other times has a hackle in a colour unique to each battalion. As with the Grenadier Guard sown on the previous page, this soldier carries the SA-80 rifle with black covers over the furniture and sight unit. (Artwork by Renato Delmaso)

11TH INFANTRY BRIGADE AND HEADQUARTERS SOUTH EAST

HQ 11th Infantry Brigade and Headquarters South East: Aldershot
1st Bn Grenadier Guards [light role infantry]: Aldershot
1st Bn Coldstream Guards [light role infantry]: Windsor
1st Bn Irish Guards [light role infantry]: Hounslow, London
1st Bn Welsh Guards [light role infantry]: Windsor
{1st Bn The Royal Gurkha Rifles [jungle role infantry]: Brunei}
{2nd Bn The Royal Gurkha Rifles [air assault infantry]: Folkstone}
{1st Bn The Royal Irish Regiment [light role infantry, now light recce strike infantry]: Tern Hill}
►Partnered with 2nd Bn The Royal Irish Regiment [light role infantry] [AR; HQ Lisburn]
3rd Bn The Princess of Wales's Royal Regiment [light role infantry] [AR; HQ Canterbury]

The 11th was redesignated from an infantry brigade to security force infantry brigade in 2021 and would reorganise with new units for the new role. HQ South-East will be separated.

Effective 4 June 2015 1st Bn Royal Gurkha Rifles was allotted to serve as a third battalion in 16th Air Assault Brigade. It shifted the assignment in Brunei with the 2nd Battalion June-July 2022.

1st Bn Royal Irish Regiment transferred from 160th Infantry Brigade 1 August 2019. Effective August 2021 the battalion was placed under command of the 16th Air Assault Brigade Combat Team. 2nd Bn of regiment also transferred from 160th Infantry Brigade 1 August 2019.

3rd Bn The Princess of Wales's Royal Regiment transferred from 7th Infantry Brigade 1 August 2019. However, it remained partnered with that brigade's 1st Bn Royal Anglian Regiment.

Soldiers from 1st Battalion the Irish Guards conducting a live firing exercise deep in the Belize Jungle during Exercise MAYAN STORM in 2016. (45162915.jpg)

51ST INFANTRY BRIGADE AND HQ SCOTLAND

HQ 51st Infantry Brigade and HQ Scotland: Edinburgh
The Royal Scots Dragoon Guards [light cavalry]: Leuchars, Fife
►Partnered with The Scottish and North Irish Yeomanry [light cavalry] [AR: RHQ Edinburgh]
The Black Watch, 3rd Bn Royal Regiment of Scotland [light role infantry]: Fort George, Inverness
►Partnered with 51st Highland Bn, 7th Bn Royal Regiment of Scotland [light role infantry] [AR; HQ Perth]
2nd Battalion The Rifles: Lisburn [light role infantry]
►Partnered with 8th Battalion The Rifles [AR; HQ Bishop Auckland]
Ceremonial and Public Duties, Scotland
Balaklava Coy, A&SH, 5th Bn Royal Regiment of Scotland: Edinburgh

The brigade HQ will transfer to Regional Command and become a purely area HQ for Scotland. Those units currently subordinated will be transferred with one exception. Balaklava Company (5 Scots) will remain on ceremonial duties under the control of the brigade.

The Scottish and North Irish Yeomanry was newly formed 31 October 2014, replacing The Royal Mercian and Lancastrian Yeomanry, which was broken up.

2nd and 8th Bns The Rifles were transferred from 38th Infantry Brigade 1 August 2019.

Soldiers from the Royal Scots Dragoon Guards (SCOTS DG) taking part in urban training at their home in Leuchars Station (RAF Leuchars), Fife in 2020. (45167617.jpg)

Military personnel lead a procession along Edinburgh's Royal Mile in July 2023. (LOS-20230705-0449-Op SCEPTRE-0199.jpg)

8 ENGINEER BRIGADE

HQ 8 Engineer Brigade: Minley
12 (Force Support) Engineer Group
HQ 12 Force Support Engineer Group: Wittering
28 Engineer Regiment [C-CBRN]
36 Engineer Regiment: Maidstone
►Partnered with 75 Engineer Regiment [AR; RHQ Warrington]
39 Engineer Regiment: Kinloss
►Partnered with 71 Engineer Regiment [AR; RHQ Leuchars, Fife]
29 EOD and Search Group
HQ 29 EOD and Search Group: Aldershot
33 Engineer Regiment (EOD and Search) [RHQ Wimbish]
35 Engineer Regiment (EOD and Search) [RHQ Wimbish]
101 (City of London) Engineer Regiment (EOD) [AR; RHQ Catford]
11 EOD Regiment RLC [RHQ Didcot]
1st Military Working Dog Regiment [Royal Army Veterinary Corps]: North Luffenham
170 (Infrastructure Support) Engineer Group
HQ 170 (Infrastructure Support) Engineer Group: Chilwell
43 HQ and Support Squadron RE: Chilwell
20 Works Group RE (Airfields): RAF Wittering
62 Works Group RE: Chilwell
63 Works Group RE: Chilwell
65 Works Group RE [AR]: Chilwell
66 Works Group RE: Chilwell

8 Engineer Brigade had been in existence since 2005 as 8 Force Engineer Brigade. It was retitled and enlarged ca August 2014.

25 (Close Support) Engineer Group

25 (Close Support) Engineer Group was organised 1 August 2014 with three engineer regiments to support the three armoured infantry brigades in the Reaction Force and two hybrid regiments to support the Adaptable Force. In 2016 the group HQ and three regiments were transferred to 3rd (UK) Division and the two hybrid regiments went into 12 (Force Support) Engineer Group. Under *Army 2020 Refine* the two hybrid regiments were reorganised as all Regular and reassigned to 25 (Close Support) Engineer Group.

29 EOD and Search Group

The group reorganised under *Army 2020 Refine*. 35 Engineer Regiment from Germany re-roled as EOD, taking over two existing EOD squadrons from 33 Regiment. All of the Army Reserve squadrons were shifted back into 101 (City of London) Engineer Regiment, which had originally been a reserve regiment; the regiment gave its two Regular squadrons to 35 Regiment.

170 (Infrastructure Support) Engineer Group

20 Works Group RE was formerly subordinated to 12 (Force Support) Group. HQ 64 Works Group RE was disbanded under *Army 2020 Refine* and several STREs shifted among the remaining works groups; no STREs were disbanded. Under *Future Soldier* the group HQ will be disbanded and the works groups moved into 12 (Force Support) Group.

A member of 11 (EOD) Regiment, Royal Logistic Corps deploying a 'Wheelbarrow Mk 8a' by moving it down a ramp form a heavily armoured six-wheeled Mastiff Protected Patrol Vehicle. The regiment were part of the Vanguard Enabling Group deployed on Exercise Shamal Storm 16 in Jordan in 2016. (45164638.jpg)

102ND LOGISTIC BRIGADE

HQ 102nd Logistic Brigade and Signal Troop (662): Grantham
6th Regiment RLC [Force Support]: Thirsk, N Yorkshire
►Partnered with 159 Supply Regiment RLC [AR; RHQ Canley]
7th Regiment RLC [Force Support]: Cottesmore
►Partnered with 158 Transport Regiment RLC [AR; RHQ Peterborough]
150 Transport Regiment RLC [AR; RHQ Hull]
1st Close Support Battalion REME: Catterick
2nd Close Support Battalion REME: Leuchars, Fife
101st Theatre Support Battalion REME [AR; HQ Keynsham]

The planned rationalisation (disbanding) of this brigade's HQ was delayed and then abandoned.

The original 101st Battalion REME was disbanded and 105th Battalion REME renumbered as 101st, with some changes to companies and locations.

Troops from 1st Battalion Royal Electrical and Mechanical Engineers conduct vehicle recovery training with Turkish Soldiers and their BMC VURAN vehicles on Exercise Steadfast Defender in 2024. (AHQCPL4-OFFICIAL-20240228-017-050.jpg)

2ND MEDICAL BRIGADE

HQ 2nd Medical Brigade: Strensall
1st Armoured Medical Regiment: Tidworth
3rd Medical Regiment: Catterick
4th Armoured Medical Regiment: Tidworth
5th Armoured Medical Regiment: Catterick
225 (Scottish) Medical Regiment [AR; RHQ Dundee]
253 (Northern Irish) Medical Regiment [AR; RHQ Belfast]
254 (East of England) Medical Regiment [AR; RHQ Cambridge]
22 Field Hospital: Nuneaton
34 Field Hospital: York to Nuneaton 2021

201 (Northern) Field Hospital [AR; HQ Newcastle]
202 (Midlands) Field Hospital [AR; HQ Birmingham]
203 (Welsh) Field Hospital [AR; HQ Cardiff]
204 (Northern Irish) Field Hospital [AR; HQ Belfast]
205 (Scottish) Field Hospital [AR; HQ Glasgow]
207 (Manchester) Field Hospital [AR; HQ Manchester]
208 (Liverpool) Field Hospital [AR; HQ Liverpool]
212 (Yorkshire) Field Hospital [AR; HQ Sheffield]
243 (Wessex) Field Hospital [AR; HQ Keynsham]
256 (City of London) Field Hospital [AR; HQ Walworth]
306 Hospital Support Regiment [AR]: Strensall
335 Medical Evacuation Regiment [AR]: Strensall

The medical regiments from 101st and 102nd Logistic Brigades were transferred to 2nd Medical Brigade. The brigade originally only had the field hospitals.

306 Hospital Support Regiment is paired with the Regular field hospitals. 335 Medical Evacuation Regiment is paired with 1st, 4th and 5th Armoured Medical Regiments. Both of these are nationally recruited regiments.

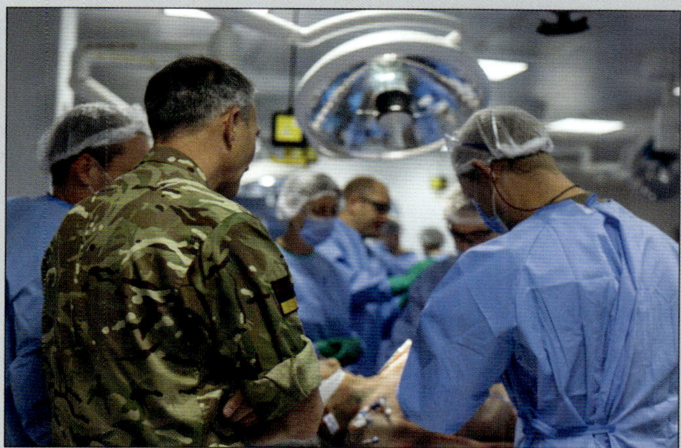

Military personnel taking part in a series of surgical simulations, including operating on cadavers. This was part of the Military Operation Specialist Team Training [MOSTT] course, which was held at the Vesalius Clinical Training Centre in Bristol, observed by a team of four senior Ukrainian clinical specialists. (DDU-Official-20230905-244-008.jpg)

6th (UK) Division

A 6th (UK) Division had most recently existed August 2008–April 2011 as a deployable HQ for service in Afghanistan (Operation Herrick). It was disbanded after that tour.

The current 6th (UK) Division began life in 2011 as Headquarters, Theatre Troops, responsible for a number of units, mostly in the UK. At the time it had 1st Artillery Brigade; 1st, 2nd and 11th Signal Brigades; 8 Force Engineer Brigade; 2nd Medical Brigade, 1st Reconnaissance Brigade; 1st Military Intelligence Brigade; and 101st, 102nd and 104th Logistic Brigades. 102nd Logistic Brigade was in Germany but had TA units that would have joined it on mobilisation.

It was reorganised under *Army 2020* as Force Troops Command (FTC), reaching full operational capability 1 April 2014. Force Troops Command was designed to deliver combat support, command support, combat services support and specialist support to the Joint, Reaction and Adaptable forces. In essence it had drawn in most of the Army outside the Royal Armoured Corps and Infantry. While some units (e.g., artillery, engineers, and logistics) were tasked for close support of the three armoured infantry brigades of the Reaction Force, they were normally under the command of a functional brigade in Force Troops Command. Some brigades were already in existence and others newly formed or reorganised as part of the *Army 2020* restructuring. Two brigades also served as regional points of command, responsible for support of all Regular and Army Reserve units within their territorial responsibility. None of the brigades were deployable: all were administrative headquarters.

On 1 August 2019 FTC was redesignated as 6th (UK) Division with a number of its subordinate brigades transferred to 1st (UK) and 3rd (UK) Divisions. In turn, it gained the Specialised Infantry Group from 1st (UK) Division. On 16 October 2020 11th Signal Brigade transferred to 3rd (UK) Division, giving up its HQ West Midlands role. The Specialised Infantry Group was redesignated as the Army Special Operations Brigade, although conversion of its British battalions to battalions of the new Ranger Regiment was delayed from August to December 2021.

During 2021 1st (UK) Signal Brigade was resubordinated to the Allied Rapid Reaction Corps.

HQ 6TH (UK) DIVISION: UPAVON

Army Special Operations Brigade

HQ, Army Special Operations Brigade: Aldershot
255 Signal Squadron: Perham Down
1st Bn Rangers [formerly Royal Scots Borderers, 1st Bn RRS]: Belfast
2nd Bn Rangers [formerly 2nd Bn Princess of Wales's Royal Regiment] s]: Aldershot
3rd Bn Rangers [formerly 2nd Bn Duke of Lancaster's Regiment]; Pirbright
4th Bn Rangers [formerly 4th Bn The Rifles]: Aldershot
Joint Counter Terrorist Training and Advisory Team: Shorncliffe

Under *Defence in a Competitive Age* the four British battalions provided the initial basis for the new Ranger Regiment. SIG was redesignated August 2021 as the Army Special Operations Brigade; its former role will be undertaken by the 11th Security Force Assistance Brigade in 1st (UK) Division. The 3rd Bn Royal Gurkha Rifles had begun recruiting in March 2020 as an additional battalion in SIG. However, with the conversion of the Specialised Infantry Group, formation of the battalion was cancelled and personnel formed into the Coriano and Falklands Companies, both of which became part of the new brigade (attached to 4th and 2nd Rangers [Army Special Operations Brigade] respectively). 255 Signal Squadron joined the brigade. 1 (Special OP) Squadron HAC [AR] will provide long-range surveillance patrols to support the brigade.

Three soldiers from 3rd Battalion, Ranger Regiment kneel in the snow looking for the enemy on an exercise in Sweden. D Company, 3rd Battalion The Ranger Regiment (3RANGERS) conducted cold weather training in Arvidsjaur, Sweden in January 2024. (AHQSGT1-OFFICIAL-20240122-003-3267.jpg)

A soldier from the Ranger Regiment poses with the new Alternative Individual Weapons (AIW) system at Lulworth Training area. An AIW system consists of: Rifle with Signature Reduction System (SRS), Magnified optic sight and Mini Red Dot (MRD) sight, and Safe Blank Firing System and Marker Round Training System. (AHQCPL12-OFFICIAL-20230713-015-009.jpg)

1ST INTELLIGENCE, SURVEILLANCE AND RECONNAISSANCE BRIGADE

HQ 1st Intelligence, Surveillance and Reconnaissance Brigade: Upavon
5th Regiment RA [Surveillance and Target Acquisition]: Catterick
4th/73rd (Sphinx) Special Observation Post Battery RA
Honourable Artillery Company [AR]: London
32nd Regiment RA: Larkhill, Salisbury [Desert Hawk UAV]
14th Signal Regiment (Electronic Warfare): Brawdry, near Haverfordwest
1st Military Intelligence Battalion [Military Intelligence]: Catterick
►Paired with 3rd Military Intelligence Battalion [AR; HQ Hackney, London]
►Also paired with 5th Military Intelligence Battalion [AR; HQ Edinburgh]
2nd Military Intelligence Battalion [Intelligence Exploitation]: Upavon
►Paired with 6th Military Intelligence Battalion [AR; HQ Manchester]
4th Military Intelligence Battalion: Bulford
►Paired with 7th Military Intelligence Battalion [AR; HQ Bristol]
Land Intelligence Fusion Centre: Hermitage
Defence Cultural Specialist Unit: Hermitage

4th/73rd (Sphinx) Special Observation Post Battery RA provides long-range patrols to identify targets for air and artillery.
32nd Regiment RA was scheduled to disband under *Army 2020 Refine*. However, on 8 October 2019 its CO announced that it would remain active in the MUAS [miniature UAS] role.

4th Military Intelligence Battalion supported 3rd (UK) Division.

A member of the Royal Regiment of Artillery during a two-week long exercise in the UK in 2017. He is shown undergoing a two-man Bergen river crossing drill. STA (Surveillance and Target Acquisition) Patrols operate at range and in close proximity to the enemy; hence their demanding selection and training needs to physically and mentally prepare them for advance force operations. (45162657.jpg)

Soldiers from the Royal Artillery assemble and fly the Desert Hawk 3 UAS (Unmanned Air System) over Salisbury Plain during a training exercise in 2014. (45157708.jpg)

77TH BRIGADE [FORMERLY SECURITY ASSISTANCE GROUP]: HERMITAGE

Defence Cultural Specialist Unit (provides behavioural analysis of actors, audiences and adversaries)
Task Group (deployable framework to deliver information and outreach)
Digital Operations Group (delivery of influence activity and products across a broad range of communication channels)
Operational Media and Communications Group (collect and analyse media content and deploy camera and communications personnel to support operations)
Outreach Group (planning support to enable outreach across military tasks and operational phases)
The Staff Corps (reservist officers, now about 100 in two groups: the General Staff and the Engineer and Logistic Staff Corps).

The Security Assistance Group was formed 1 September 2014. It was renamed 77th Brigade (commemorating the Chindit 77th Indian Infantry Brigade of the Second World War) in January 2015; the 77th operated behind Japanese lines in Burma. In July 2015 the existing components (Military Stabilisation and Support Group, the Media Operations Group, 15 Psychological Operations Group and the Security Capacity Building team) were redesignated as columns. (Infantry battalions in the Second World War brigade were each divided into two columns for operations). However, the column designations have now been dropped. This is a combined organisation of Regular and Army Reserve personnel; many elements are largely reservists.

The Staff Corps, formerly separate, was added in October 2015. The General Staff group is composed of senior level managers with expertise in technical communications, corporate strategies, advertising, marketing, digital commerce, banking and academia. Presumably their commissions are in the General Service Corps. The Engineer and Logistic Staff Corps was formerly a separate group of 60 non-deployable Reservist advisors (10 colonels, 20 lieutenant colonels and 30 majors) with senior business experience in engineering, logistics, communications and commercial matters. All are given Reserve commissions in the Royal Engineers. They provide expert advice and specialist knowledge to operations and training.

4
ROYAL MARINES AND THE ROYAL NAVY

With the Army cut from the pre-*Army 2020* seven brigades, the Royal Marines' 3rd Commando Brigade formed an even larger part of the available British ground troops. However, only two Commandos (40 and 45) are still in the traditional amphibious light infantry role, and that will be altered under Future Commando Force. The Army has always provided the artillery and engineers for the brigade, along with some support units. Army personnel must pass the RM commando training course and earn the green beret before assignment. The RM also provides the Special Boat Service (SBS) to UK Special Forces. The current Commandant General, from November 2022, is General Gwyn Jenkins CB, OBE, ADC. He has also been Vice-Chief of the Defence Staff since August 2022. His predecessor, from April 2021, was Lieutenant General Robert Magowan CB, CBE. He has been Deputy Chief of the Defence Staff (Financial and Military Capability) since May 2022. Prior to that he had been Deputy Commander, Strategic Command. He was the first lieutenant general to hold the Commandant General post; previously that was a two-star position.

A proposal to restructure the Royal Marines was announced in April 2017, termed the Commando Forces 2030 strategy, also known as the Future Commando Force. The new structure will include two littoral response groups (built in part from the two amphibious commandos), one based east of Suez (LRG South) and one in the High North (LRG North). These changes form part of a coherent attempt to integrate the Royal Marines into the mainstream of the Royal Navy. A Vanguard (i.e. initial, or test) Strike Company (VSC) of around 150 RM and Army personnel was formed in autumn 2020. A strike company is expected to work in small teams tailored for particular missions. Some sources indicate that each LRG will have a strike company, serving six-month tours.

The Littoral Response Group (Experimentation) deployed September 2020 to the Mediterranean, Black Sea and North Africa for a three-month test of the concept. It had over 1,000 RN and RM personnel and drew on 40, 42, 30 and 47 Commandos, supported by Wildcat helicopters.

LRG North was deployed in 2021. It is intended for use in European/northern waters. As of June 2021 it was operational in the Baltic with HMS *Albion* (a landing platform dock) to carry the Marines (personnel from 45 Commando and supporting elements), the frigate HMS *Lancaster*, the RFA vessel *Mounts Bay* (an auxiliary landing ship dock),[4] and helicopters from 847 Naval Air Squadron. LRG North is intended to operate in the Atlantic, Baltic, Arctic Ocean and the Mediterranean. LRG South would be based in Oman and operate in the Persian Gulf and Indo-Pacific theatre. The two commandos will be reorganised into four strike companies.

LRG South formed in September 2023 with RFA *Argus* (primarily a casualty ship) and RFA *Lyme Bay* (a landing platform dock) along with personnel from 40 Commando and supporting units. It deployed to the Mediterranean the next month. They then moved to the Red Sea and then made stops India and Australia.

In March 2023 the RM established Camp Viking near Skjold in northern Norway. This serves as a base for winter warfare training for the next 10 years, as well as a depot for vehicles, weapons and equipment.

Pictured are 40 Commando conducting a raid after deploying from an Inflatable Raiding Craft (IRC) of 539 Assault Squadron who are part of 47 Commando during Winter Deployment 2022. (FLEET-20220216-AJ0001-130.jpg)

A covert insertion exercise of a team from 45 Commando by inflatable raiding craft from 47 Commando before moving to a target location in Lithuania during Op BATAN in 2021. (45168764.jpg)

Bravo Company, 40 Commando Royal Marines having completed their final strike onto enemy positions during Exercise Olympus Warrior in 2020 as part of LRG(X) in Cyprus. The Marines successfully received Bergan drops from Malloy Aeronautics heavy lift aircraft. (45167322.jpg)

Royal Marines of Bravo Company 40 Commando conducting advance to contact live firing serial whilst deployed on LRG(X) in Cyprus in 2020. LRG(X) will operate from Royal Navy shipping to provide forward presence in the Mediterranean, North Africa, the Levant and Black Sea, focusing training and operations with NATO and regional partners whilst developing experimentation (X) and innovation trials that underpin the Littoral Strike concept, the Future Commando Force vision and the Royal Navy's Transformation strategy. (AJ200009188.jpg)

3RD COMMANDO BRIGADE

30 Commando Information Exploitation [IX] Group: Plymouth
- 30 Commando Headquarters
- Surveillance and Reconnaissance Squadron
- Y Squadron [EW], including Air Defence Troop
- Communications Squadron
- Logistics Squadron, including RM Police Troop
- Base Squadron

40 Commando: Taunton: provides the strike teams for LRG South
45 Commando: RM Condor (Scotland): provides the strike teams for LRG North
Armoured Support Group: Bovington
29th Commando Regiment RA [105mm Light Gun]: Plymouth
148th (Meiktila) Commando Battery RA: Poole
289th Commando Artillery Troop [UAV] [AR]: Plymouth
24 Commando Engineer Regiment: Chivenor
Commando Logistic Regiment: Chivenor
- HQ Squadron
- Equipment Support Squadron
- Logistic Support Squadron
- Medical Squadron
- Landing Force Support Squadron
- Logistic Task Group
- 383 Commando Petroleum Troop RLC [AR]: Plymouth

539 Raiding Squadron: HMNB Devonport, Plymouth
47 Commando (Raiding Group): RM Tamar, Devonport
- 10 (Landing Craft) Training Squadron: RM Tamar, HMNB Devonport (Plymouth)
- 11 Amphibious Trials and Training Squadron: Instow, North Devon
- Also serves as parent unit for:
  - 4 Assault Squadron: Plymouth: serves on HMS *Bulwark* (L15)
  - 6 Assault Squadron, Plymouth: serves on HMS *Albion* (L14)

42 Commando, Bickleigh, Devon, was reorganised May 2018 into specialised companies. Juliet Company is trained for boarding operations; Kilo Company provides support, augmentation, liaison and training; Lima Company is tasked for rescue operations; and Mike Company provides force protection for RN and RFA ships.

43 Commando, HM Naval Base Clyde, is termed the Fleet Protection Group. In fact, its role is to provide security for the RN's nuclear weapons. O and P Squadrons provide waterfront nuclear security; R Squadron provides nuclear security on the Clyde.

There is one reserve unit, the 2nd Raiding Squadron, at Plymouth. HQ and Signal Squadron, 3rd Commando Brigade, was later redesignated United Kingdom Landing Force Command Support Group (UKLF CSG) and then in 2010 given the 30 Commando designation. No 30 Commando in the Second World War was intended to operate with forward units to seize documents or other material.

The Armoured Support Group, formed in December 2007, commemorates the 1944 RM Armoured Support Group (tanks mounted on LCTs) used to provide fire support for the Normandy landings. It operates Viking All Terrain Vehicles (Protected). It was formed from the RM Armoured Support Company (Afghanistan) and the RM Viking Training Squadron. There does not seem to be any information on the exact organisation of this unit; the RM have 99 Viking vehicles.

539 Raiding Squadron controls a variety of craft: LCVP, Hovercrafts, and Rigid Raider small craft. Per its web page it can also operate the Viking amphibious vehicles. It was renamed in November 2019 from 539 Assault Squadron when 1 Assault Group redesignated as 47 Commando.

47 Commando (Raiding Group) was formed 5 November 2019 by redesignation of 1 Assault Group Royal Marines and placed under 3rd Commando Brigade. Each assault squadron has four LCUs and four LCVPs.

Organisation and Equipment

A normal Royal Marine commando has six companies and a strength of 638 personnel. The command company has the HQ along with recce (ISTAR), mortar, and signal troops. The logistic company has all of the support personnel. There are four other companies. Each has two troops (28 personnel each) and a fire support group (25 personnel). The latter has a GPMG detachment and three detachments which can have Javelin ATGW, HMGs or grenade MGs depending on the mission. This can be expected to change as 40 and 45 Commandos reorganise to provide strike teams for the littoral response groups.

The RM also contribute a company to the Special Forces Support Group.

The Viking BvS10 All Terrain Armoured Vehicle is a twin-cab articulated amphibious tracked vehicle, similar to the Bv 206, although larger and armoured. It has a 7.62mm MG in a ring mount on the first cab. There are four variants: Troop Carrying Vehicle (two crew and up to 10 passengers), Command Variant (two crew and up to eight passengers), Repair and Recovery Variant (four fitters

Viking armoured vehicles from Viking Mortar Section of Armoured Support Group firing their mortars in 2020. (45167544.jpg & 45167544.jpg)

LCVP loading and unloading serials using Viking Amphibious Vehicles in the High North of Norway during Ex STEADFAST DEFENDER in 2024. The UK Commando Force has been exercising in the High North, working with partner nations in Norway and surrounding area. (DDU_062_20240227_NORWAY- LCVP Viking Dise (2).jpg)

The new Commando Raiding Craft (CRC) in Plymouth Sound as the replacement for the Offshore Raiding Craft (ORC), being demonstrated by 47 Commando (Raiding Group) Royal Marines in February 2024. (FRPUW-20240207-XV0116-131.jpg)

HMS *Albion* arrives in The Netherlands in June 2023. Alongside is a Landing Craft Vehicle Personnel (LCVP). (45170520.jpg)

A Royal Navy Merlin helicopter overflies a Royal Marine Landing craft during an Olympic security exercise near Weymouth, Dorset in 2012. (45154029.jpg)

and a crane and other equipment), and the Ambulance Variant. The vehicle can be carried underneath a Chinook or divided into the two sections with each carried underneath a Merlin. The RM accepted 108 vehicles beginning in 2005 and 99 were upgraded by 2016. A proposal to replace them with a new All Terrain Military Vehicle (Support) back in 2008–2009 was later cancelled. However, the UK has joined Germany and Sweden in an order for the improved Bv410 Viking. This has better armour, improved land mine protection, and can carry more troops or cargo. It is amphibious. This version is known as the Collaborative All Terrain Vehicle (CATV).

Royal Navy

The RN has two Landing Platform Docks, HMS *Albion* (pennant L14) and HMS *Bulwark* (pennant L15); these are different from the similarly roled RFA vessels. These entered service in 2003 and 2004, but the designations are traditional for the role, beginning with former light fleet carriers completed after the Second World War and later adapted to carry RM commandos and helicopters. Their normal capacity is 405 Royal Marines, but they can carry 710 on overload. The vessels can also carry up to 67 vehicles, depending on the type, or 30 of the armoured Vikings. Each carries four LCU Mk 10 (Landing Craft Utility) and four LCVP Mk 5 (Landing Craft Vehicle and Personnel). There are two landing spots for helicopters up to the size of a Chinook.

The LCU Mk 10 has a crew of seven and can carry 120 troops or four lorries or one MBT. Deliveries began in 1998 to replace the older Mk 9, and the RN has 10 in total. The LCVP Mk 5 has a crew of three and can carry 35 troops. They entered service from 1996 to replace the older Mk 4. The RN has 19 in service of the 23 originally built.

RFA *Mounts Bay* in Norway. As part of Nordic Response 24, RFA *Mounts Bay* was deployed in the Artic Circle in Norway carrying personnel from the Commando Force, including Royal Marine, Army and Navy Commandos, along with Army, Navy and RAF personnel. (DDU-20240305-54-RFA Mounts Bay-009.jpg)

This gives them two LCUs and 11 LCVPs in addition to the eight of each carried on the two LPDs. The craft carried on the LPDs are all manned by the Royal Marines. It is probable that the remainder are also crewed by Marines as other parts of 47 Commando (Raiding Group).

An auxiliary landing ship dock, like RFA *Mounts Bay*, is a replacement for earlier logistics ships. They can carry 356 soldiers, 24 tanks or 150 light trucks. The well dock can carry one LCU Mk 10 or two LCVPs, along with two Mexeflote landing rafts hung on the sides. Cargo capacity is 200 tons of ammunition or 24 containers. There are three of these ships. The standard sized Mexeflote raft has a crew of six and can carry 130,000 lbs of cargo.

5
JOINT HELICOPTER COMMAND

When 16th Air Assault Brigade left the Joint Helicopter Command in 2015, 7th Air Assault Battalion REME was detached from the brigade and came under Joint Helicopter Command 30 November 2015. 47th Regiment RA [Watchkeeper UAS] transferred to JHC in August 2016.

1st Aviation Brigade was established 1 April 2020 at Wattisham, combining Wattisham Flying Station Headquarters (formerly the Attack Helicopter Force) and the Aviation Reconnaissance Force at RNAS Yeovilton. HQ is now at Middle Wallop. It was expected to be operational on creation, but to only reach initial operating capability 1 April 2021 and full operating capability January 2023. It commanded all of the AAC regiments and 7th Air Assault Battalion REME from the outset, gaining 47th Regiment RA by April 2021. Redesignated 1 October 2022 as 1st Aviation Brigade Combat Team. It was then expected to reach full operational capability by 1 April 2023.

7th Aviation Battalion REME: Wattisham
47th Regiment RA [Watchkeeper KW450 UAS]: Larkhill, Wilts

ARMY AIR CORPS

1 Regiment AAC [multi-role light utility helicopter: Wildcat AH1]: RNAS Yeovilton
3 Regiment AAC [Apache AH-64E]: Wattisham
4 Regiment AAC [Apache AH1]: Wattisham
653 Squadron AAC [Apache AH1 OCU] [Sometimes shown as under the operational control of 3 Regiment AAC]
5 Regiment AAC [Gazelle AH1]: Aldergrove, NI
6 Regiment AAC [AR] provides trained groundcrew reinforcements for the Regular regiments

25 Flight AAC: Middle Wallop [under administrative control of 671 Squadron/7 (Training) Regiment AAC

3 Regiment AAC was reduced to two squadrons under *Army 2020*, with its 653 Squadron AAC becoming the Apache operational conversion unit and separated. Tasked to support 3rd (UK) Division. It began to operate with new AH-64E autumn 2022. The regiment was declared ready for operations after a six-week field exercise in October 2023.

4 Regiment AAC was also reduced to two squadrons under *Army 2020*, with its 654 Squadron AAC disbanded. Tasked to support 16th Air Assault Brigade and 3rd RM Commando Brigade.

Apache AH-64E attack helicopter's start rotors ready for take-off from Wattisham Airfield for Exercise Steadfast Defender on 24 April 2024. (APOSEC-OFFICIAL-20240424-013-0022.jpg)

An Apache AH-64E attack helicopter is refuelled on the apron by soldiers from the 4 Regiment Army Air Corps to be prepared for flight for Exercise Steadfast Defender 24, 23 April 2024. (APOSEC-OFFICIAL-20240423-013-0078.jpg)

An AAC Wildcat AH1 flying, with two new Apache AH-64E aircraft on the ground during Exercise Steadfast Defender 24. (HON-20240424-064-Ex Swift Response-0699.jpg)

RAF HELICOPTER FORCE

RAF Odiham (Hampshire)
- 7 Squadron [Chinook HC2]
- 18 Squadron [Chinook HC2]
- 27 Squadron [Chinook HC2]

RAF Benson (South Oxfordshire)
- 28 Squadron [Chinook HC4 and Puma HC2]
- 33 Squadron [Puma HC2]
- 230 Squadron [Puma HC1]

The RAF also has 84 Squadron (Griffin HAR2, replaced in 2023 by Puma HC2) at Akrotiri, Cyprus, and, from 2022, 1563 Flight in Brunei with the Puma HC2.

RAF Benson was the site of two squadrons equipped with the Merlin HC3/3a. However, these were turned over to the Fleet Air Arm: 78 Squadron gave its Merlins to 846 Naval Air Squadron 1 October 2014 and 28 Squadron turned over the last RAF Merlins to 845 Naval Air Squadron 10 July 2015. The former squadron was disbanded and the latter assumed a new role. After handing over the Merlins to the RNAS in July 2015, 28 Squadron became the combined operational conversion unit for the Puma and Chinook.

Chinooks and Apaches AH-64E line up on the runway at Amari Air Base, ready to launch a coordinated assault during Exercise Swift Response, part of Exercise Steadfast Defender in May 2024. (2024-SKL-005-148.jpg)

A Puma of 84 Squadron based at Royal Air Force Akrotiri in Cyprus in March 2023. (AKR-20230331-113-84 Sqn Handover-Take Over-157.jpg)

ROYAL NAVY COMMANDO HELICOPTER FORCE

The primary role of this Force is to provide rotary wing support to 3rd Commando Brigade RM. The two lift squadrons were modernised 2014–15 by taking over the Merlin HC3 helicopters from the RAF.

RNAS Yeovilton (Somerset)
- 845 Naval Air Squadron [Merlin HC3/3a/4]
- 846 Naval Air Squadron [Merlin HC3/3a]
- 847 Naval Air Squadron [Wildcat AH1]

Personnel from 7 Battery RHA conduct helicopter under slung load training along with Merlin's from 845 Naval Air Squadron during Steadfast Defender in 2024. (DDU-20240227-049-NORWAY- Helicopter Under (2).jpg)

The Commando Mobile Air Operations Team (CDO MAOT) working with the MAOT team from the Joint Helicopter Support Squadron carry out load lifting training with a Wildcat AH1 helicopter of 847 Naval Air Squadron (845 NAS) in the snowy mountains around Bardufoss in northern Norway. (FLEET-20240206-XD0071-014.jpg)

Squadron Badges

RAF squadrons all have distinct squadron badges. These consist of a circle in RAF blue with thin golden edges and an outer border of gold laurel leaves, ensigned by the Queen's (St. Edward's) Crown and above a scroll (gold) with a motto in black. (The Queen's Crown will be replaced by the Imperial or Tudor Crown, sometimes called the King's Crown.) For numbered units there are indentations on each side of the circle. The white interior of the circle contains a distinctive image. The top of the circle has 'Squadron' in black and the lower half has 'Royal Air Force' in black. The indented numbers are in black. 230 Squadron, for example, has a tiger in front of a palm tree, and the motto 'Kiti chari jauh' (We search far), all reflecting their association with Malaya prior to 1938.

The Army Air Corps squadrons, many of which were originally formed in the RAF, have the same type of squadron badge. The difference is that the top also has 'Squadron' in black but the bottom reads 'Army Air Corps' in black. 651 Squadron, for example, has a yellow seashell with red flames and the motto 'Dirige' (Direct).

Naval air squadrons have a completely different stye of badge. These are circles enclosed with a golden-brown rope and a rectangle above with the squadron number in black. Above the squadron number is a naval crown in golden-brown. The centre of the badge contains a distinctive image. These centres can be white or in other colours and may include representations of waves in blue. 847 Naval Air Squadron, for example, has a sea lion (gold from arms and wings upward, blue-grey below) on a blue background.

6
ARMY ELEMENT JOINT FORCES [STRATEGIC] COMMAND

42 Engineer Regiment (Geographic): Wyton [includes an AR squadron]
Defence Human Intelligence Command: Chicksands

United Kingdom Special Forces

All UK Special Forces (UKSF) come under the Director, Special Forces in Strategic Command. While within Strategic Command, the Director, Special Forces reports directly to the Chief of the Defence Staff. Candidates for the Special Air Service can be any member of the Armed Forces; only the reserve elements recruit from the general public. Training is at Sennybridge and the Brecon Beacons in Wales.

The new Ranger Regiment, when fully operational, will support the SAS by undertaking some of the operations they performed, allowing the SAS to spend more time working with MI6 in covert operations worldwide. The Rangers were established December 2021, with four battalions as part of the new Army Special Operations Brigade. While its initial basis was the four British battalions of the Specialised Infantry Group, it will be open to anyone in the armed forces. Each battalion will be around 250 personnel. It will be routinely deployed to train and support allied nations. The four Ranger battalions will be joined in the brigade by the Joint Counter Terrorist Training and Advisory Team (JCTTAT). According to the British Army web site, 'The Ranger Battalions will consist of All Arms Regular and Reserve volunteers who are carefully screened, assessed, selected and then professionally educated and trained prior to deploying on operations.' However, the regiment itself remains part of 6th (UK) Division rather than UK Special Forces.

Army

22 SAS Regiment: Hereford
21 SAS Regiment (Artists) [AR; RHQ Duke of York's Barracks, London]
23 SAS Regiment [AR; RHQ Birmingham]

- **Special Reconnaissance Regiment: Hereford**

Formed in April 2005, built around 14 Intelligence Company, which had served in Northern Ireland. It is intended for surveillance and counter-terrorism, relieving the SAS of that role, and is believed to be company-sized (150 personnel). It can recruit from all of the armed services.

- **Special Forces Support Group [1st Bn The Parachute Regiment]: St Athan, Wales**

Created in April 2006, the SFSG provides specialist infantry support to special forces, such as the SAS. Personnel from the other parachute battalions rotate through this unit during their careers. RM personnel are now spread throughout the unit instead of being concentrated in F Company. The RAF Regiment also contributes a platoon, along with forward air controllers. It was originally built around 1st Bn Parachute Regiment, which is no longer considered to be a formed unit in the Army.

- **18th (United Kingdom Special Forces) Signal Regiment: Hereford**

Aviation

Joint Special Forces Aviation Wing: RAF Odiham
658 Squadron AAC: Hereford
Special Forces flight, 7 Squadron: RAF Odiham [Chinook HC4]
Special Forces flight, 47 Squadron: RAF Brize Norton [C-130J]
Maritime Interdiction Flight, 815 Naval Air Squadron: RNAS Yeovilton [Lynx HMA8]

658 Squadron AAC was until September 2013 the independent No 8 Flight. It had four August A109 helicopters (two new and two captured from Argentina). It then had a mix of AS365 N3 Dauphin helicopters in civilian colours and the Gazelle AH1 (three according to some sources). The Maritime Interdiction Flight operates two helicopters with aircrew and engineer technicians. It was formerly designated B Section. The bulk of the squadron operates Lynx HMA8 helicopters carried on some destroyers and frigates.

Royal Marines

Special Boat Service: RM Base Poole [four squadrons]

Originally C and X Squadrons specialised in canoe and small boat operations; Z Squadron were divers; and M Squadron trained for maritime anti-terrorism on ships, oil rigs, etc. However, all squadrons now rotate through counter-terrorism duties. SBS has been estimated to number 200–250 personnel. While staffed largely from the RM commandos, personnel of any service can volunteer for the unit.

A Mk 4 Chinook helicopter takes off from RAF Odiham during a testing exercise. The first upgraded Royal Air Force (RAF) Chinook Mk4 helicopters (HC4) deployed to Afghanistan in late November 2012, less than six months after their introduction to frontline squadrons. Under Project Julius, the entire RAF Chinook fleet was to be upgraded with the Thales digital 'glass' cockpit procured through prime contractor Boeing, together with upgraded Honeywell T-55-714 engines. In turn, by February 2022 the HC4 had itself been replaced and the Chinook fleet now consists of HC5, HC6 and HC6A variants. (45155110.jpg)

Pictured is a Hercules C-130J from 47 Squadron, (accompanied by a Typhoon) on a final flypast before its retirement. Since entering RAF service, originally with 242 Operational Conversion Unit at RAF Thorney Island, the Hercules operated across the globe in support of UK military and humanitarian relief operations. The transition to the 22-strong Atlas (A400) fleet and other air mobility aircraft had been ongoing for some time before the final retirement of the RAF's Hercules fleet in June 2023. (ACSSU-20230614-0092-Herc Final Tour-0012.jpg)

7
RAF REGIMENT AND RAF FORCE PROTECTION

The RAF Regiment is the force protection element of the RAF. The regiment's squadrons are under 2 Group, which is responsible for air transport and aerial refuelling, ISTAR, and force protection. From 2011–2019 the RAF Regiment assumed responsibility for CBRN (Chemical, biological, radiological and nuclear) defence from the former Joint CBRN Regiment (formed from 1st Royal Tank Regiment and 27 Squadron, RAF Regiment). One squadron remained in the role until 2021. RAF Regiment personnel also serve with the Special Forces Support Group. Other ranks in the RAF Regiment are referred to as Gunners.

AIR FORCE PROTECTION [FIELD] SQUADRONS:

1 Squadron: RAF Honington, Suffolk {7 Force Protection Wing}
II Squadron:[5] RAF Brize Norton, Oxfordshire {4 Force Protection Wing}
15 Squadron: RAF Marham, Norfolk {3 Force Protection Wing}
34 Squadron: RAF Leeming, North Yorkshire {2 Force Protection Wing
51 Squadron: RAF Lossiemouth, Moray {5 Force Protection Wing}
63 Squadron (King's Colour Squadron): RAF Northolt, Middlesex {2 Force Protection Wing}

CBRN Squadron:

27 Squadron: RAF Honington, Suffolk: disbanded October 2021

The reserve element is known as the Royal Auxiliary Air Force Regiment:
603 (City of Edinburgh) Squadron [one flight only] [5 Force Protection Wing]
609 (West Riding) Squadron: RAF Leeming [2 Force Protection Wing]
2503 (County of Lincoln) Squadron: RAF Waddington [8 Force Protection Wing]
2620 (County of Norfolk) Squadron: RAF Marham [3 Force Protection Wing]
2622 (Highland) Squadron: RAF Lossiemouth [5 Force Protection Wing]
2623 (East Anglian) Squadron: RAF Honington [7 Force Protection Wing]
2624 (County of Oxfordshire) Squadron: RAF Prize Norton [4 Force Protection Wing]

Field (force protection) squadrons are somewhat larger than an Army rifle company, with 170–175 personnel. They are organised into rifle flights (platoons) and a support weapons flight (mortars, MGs, and snipers). The two squadrons once identified as light armoured appear to have converted to field squadrons.

When C-CBRN responsibility was transferred back to the Army, No 20 Wing and 26 Squadron RAF Regiment were disbanded. 27 Squadron was under the Army's 28 Regiment RE until it was also disbanded.

RAF Force Protection Force HQ is at RAF Honington. The RAF has a number of so-called force protection wings:

No. 2 Force Protection Wing: RAF Leeming
No. 3 Force Protection Wing: RAF Marham
No. 4 Force Protection Wing: RAF Brize Norton
No. 5 Force Protection Wing: RAF Lossiemouth
No. 7 Force Protection Wing: RAF Coningsby
No. 8 Force Protection Wing: RAF Waddington

These had elements of the RAF Regiment, EOD personnel, Intelligence and others to provide policing and ground defence. These formations were formerly known as Survive to Operate HQs and they are deployable. Some had assigned RAF Police squadrons. However, it does not appear that any RAF Police squadrons remain assigned to force protection wings.

No. 8 Force Protection Wing does not have an RAF Regiment squadron assigned. However, 1, 4, 5 and 6 RAF Police Squadrons are shown as assigned on its web page.

Most of the force protection wings (all but No 7) had an RAF Police squadron assigned. However, as of 2023 the RAF Police have been reorganised and their squadrons are grouped under three police and security wings.

No. 8 Force Protection Wing does not have an RAF Regiment squadron assigned. However, 1, 4, 5 and 6 RAF Police Squadrons are shown as assigned on its web page.

Most of the force protection wings (all but No. 7) had an RAF Police squadron assigned. However, as of 2023 the RAF Police have been reorganised and their squadrons are grouped under three police and security wings.

The RAF Police began a reorganization in 2021–22 to more tightly align their squadrons with operating forces (e.g., Air Mobility Force, Lightning Force, Typhoon Force) as well as reorganise units to meet current and future threats. The new wing headquarters would align with RAF groups. A planned three-year makeover, it began with Police from Nos 4 and 8 Protection Wings. The reorganised RAF Police were grouped into three wings and nine squadrons, mostly retitled as police and security. This removed them from the existing force protection wings. However, this was at least partially reversed in 2022. The RAF web site does not list wings, so it is not

RAF Regiment CBRN Team personnel pictured analysing samples during Exercise Olympus Cloud at RAF Akrotiri, Cyprus. These Teams provide COUNTER-CHEMICAL, BIOLOGICAL, RADIOLOGICAL AND NUCLEAR (C-CBRN) SUPPORT. This includes specialist C-CBRN support to UK Defence, including point and area reconnaissance for CBRN hazards including lethal nerve agents such as Sarin and VX, biological agents such as Anthrax and potentially hazardous radiological sources. (45169472.jpg)

clear if these police and security wings were formed and, if so, still exist or were disbanded. None of the web pages for the RAF Police squadrons refers to a police and security wing.

The former police and security wings were described as 1 ('People' facing), 2 ('Platform' facing) and 3 ('Air Mobility' facing).

The Specialist Police Wing at RAF Honington controls various specialist entities (Special Investigation Branch, Force Protection Intelligence Center, Forensic Exploitation Flight, Counter Intelligence and Security Sqn) along with 3 Tactical Police Sqn.[6]

The squadrons are:

1 Tactical Police and Security Sqn: supports the Air Mobility Force when deployed. RAF Brize Norton.

2 RAF Police Counter Intelligence and Security Sqn. RAF Honington.

3 RAF Police (Reserve) Sqn: reservist support to operations. RAF Honington.

4 RAF Police (Typhoon) Sqn: supports the Typhoon Force. RAF Lossiemouth.

5 RAF Police (ISTAR) Sqn: supports the ISTAR Force. RAF Waddington.

6 RAF Police (Lightning) Sqn: responsible for middle England RAF units (Norfolk to the Welsh border). RAF Marham.

7 RAF Police (Air Mobility) Security Sqn supporting the bases of the Air Mobility Force.

8 RAF Police and Security Sqn: supports the 22 Group training establishments. RAF Cranwell.

9 RAF Police and Security Sqn: supports the Battlespace Management Force and UK Space Force. RAF High Wycombe.

Squadron Badges

Squadrons of the RAF Regiment, like flying units, have distinctive squadron badges. These consist of a circle in RAF blue with thin golden edges and an outer border of gold laurel leaves, ensigned by the Queen's (St. Edward's) Crown and above a scroll (gold) with a motto in black. The Queen's Crown will be replaced in due course. For numbered units there are indentations on each side of the circle. The white interior of the circle contains a distinctive image. These have 'Squadron' in black or gold at the top of the circle, 'Royal Air Force Regiment' in black or gold at the bottom of the circle, and the squadron number in black or gold on the indents. 51 Squadron, for example, has a cheetah in full stride in front of a curved sword with a notched blade. The motto 'Celeriter defendere' (Swift to defend) is in black.

The Regiment itself has a badge. This has 'Royal Air Force Regiment' in black around the blue circle, with a gold laurel wreath at the base, and the motto 'Per Ardua' (Through adversity) in black. The central device is crossed rifles passing through a gold Saxon crown.

The Royal Air Force Police also have a distinctive badge. This has 'Royal Air Force Police' in gold around the blue circle, with three black dots at the bottom. The central device is a gold griffin. The motto 'Fiat Justitia' (Let justice be done) is in black.

Members of the RAF's 1 Squadron Force Protection seen on exercise in Cyprus in 2022. (AKR-20220628-225-1 Sqn FP Ex Epi Dry Range-304.jpg)

A Military Working Dog with RAF Police handler on patrol during the Bitework element of the Military Working Dog Trials in November 2022. Throughout the trials, competitors were tested in a variety of operational scenarios including core skills of agility and obedience, threat perception during day and night patrols, and a dog's ability to track and trace intruders through wind scent capabilities. Military Working Dogs provide a pivotal capability that supports the protection and enablement of Air and Space Power. (HON-20221108-235-MWD-191.jpg and HON-20221108-235-MWD-108.jpg)

Members of 15 Squadron RAF Regiment respond to a staged attack on a mock Afghan Police Station at the Stanford Training Area (STANTA) in Norfolk during the final exercise in March 2014 before deploying to Afghanistan. (45157187.jpg)

8
MISCELLANEOUS OVERSEAS DEPLOYMENTS

The British Army maintains two sovereign base areas in Cyprus – Dhekelia and Episkopi – with about 2,400 personnel total. Light role battalions from the Adaptable Force serve two-year rotations, reduced from three under *Army 2020*. 7th Infantry Brigade handled rotations for Dhekelia (most recently 1st Bn The Rifles in July 2023) and 4th Infantry Brigade handled rotations for Episkopi (most recently 1st Bn Duke of Lancaster's Regiment in July 2022). In the future, however, rotations will be of light mechanised battalions from 7th Light Mechanised Brigade Combat Team. There are very small support units at each, including 234 Signal Squadron, part of the Joint Service Signal Unit, Cyprus. There are also personnel from the Royal Logistic Corps, Royal Army Medical Corps, Royal Electrical and Mechanical Engineers, and Royal Military Police. Cyprus formerly also had an engineer squadron and AAC flight but both have been disbanded. Separately, some British Army personnel serve six-month roulement tours with the United Nations Force in Cyprus, manning the boundary between the Greek and Turkish held areas. There is no relationship between the sovereign base areas and the UN deployment. That is referred to as Op Tosca by the UK.

There is a small force in Brunei: about 700 personnel, mainly a Gurkha battalion and, formerly, an AAC flight with Bell 212 helicopters. The two battalions of The Royal Gurkha Rifles serve

A soldier of 24 Commando RE participating in Ex AUSTERE WOLF working a wire obstacle on the Akrotiri Mole in 2022. (AKR-20221003-342-Ex Austere Wolf-0079.jpg)

A member of 2 Para, 16 Air Assault Brigade, participating in an exercise on Cyprus in 2021. (APOSEC-Official-20210614-014-025.jpg)

Forbidden Zone sign in the Buffer Zone of Nicosia, Cyprus, photographed in 2018. British troops are part of the United Nations Peace Keeping Force in Cyprus (UNFICYP), working out of Wolseley Barracks in Nicosia and cover patrol missions through the Buffer Zone which separates northern and south areas of Cyprus. The Buffer Zone – also called 'the Green Line' – extends approximately 180km across the island. In some parts of old Nicosia, it is only a few meters wide, while in other areas it is a few kilometres wide. Its northern and southern limits are the lines where the belligerents stood following the ceasefire of 16 August 1974, as recorded by UNFICYP. (45166003.jpg)

rotating three-year tours. The AAC squadron with Bell 212 helicopters was disbanded in 2022 and replaced by an RAF flight. The Jungle Warfare Division there runs courses for the Army.

The British Army Training Unit Suffield (BATUS) at Alberta, Canada, includes 29 (BATUS) Flight AAC and 105 Logistic Support Squadron RLC. BATUS is equipped with in excess of 1,000 vehicles including a full complement of Challenger 2 tanks and Warrior Infantry Fighting Vehicles. More than 400 permanent staff and 1,000 temporary deployed staff. The area is some 2,700 square km and armoured battle group train there.

The largest overseas deployment had been the remaining elements in Germany, but these returned to the UK by 2019. Personnel are now located at Paderborn (Normandy and Athlone Barracks). There is the Sennelager Training Centre with some 2,700 square km. The Monchengladbach vehicle storage depot has in excess of 1,000 vehicles (including Challenger 2 MBTs and Warrior IFVs) stored for use in training exercises. There is also the Wulfen munitions storage depot. The M3 amphibious rigs of 23 Squadron RE are at Minden. The local permanent staff are around 400 personnel. Five combined arms battlegroups undergo 30-day training sessions each year, including live firing.

In 2016 NATO established an extended Forward Presence in the Baltic states and Poland. The British are the lead in Estonia under the rubric of Operation Cabrit. About 900 personnel serve rotational tours, alongside personnel from other NATO states. This is normally a Warrior battalion, along with a tank squadron. Some helicopters were deployed as well in 2019 and are occasionally sent out for exercises. Later, the UK sent an element to the US-led force in Poland. This is an armoured cavalry or light cavalry squadron, and there are around 150 personnel involved on these rotations. However, an additional 350 personnel were sent out in February 2022 when elements of 45 RM Commando deployed on an exercise. The RM now have a base in Norway to support training and operations there.

The British Army Training Unit Kenya (BATUK) is mainly based at Nanyuki. A small staff there (around 100 personnel, with a reinforcing cohort of 280 on short tours) supports periodic infantry battalion and Royal Engineer exercises in that nation. Under a treaty with Kenya, up to six infantry battalions can engage in eight-week exercises.

Elsewhere in Africa, 300 British personnel participated in Op Newcombe in support of the UN mission in Mali prior to a decline in relations between the British (and other Western governments) and Mali's government, and the ending of that mission announced in November 2022. Training is conducted in Somalia under UN and EU auspices, and the Army provides security training and medical support elsewhere in Africa.

There is a British Army Training Support Unit in Belize (BATSUB) with 12 permanent personnel and 100 civilians. Various training exercises are conducted there, including the British Army Platoon Commander Battle Course.

A small multi-service force is still stationed in the Falkland Islands. RA and RE personnel serve six-month tours; the former includes an air defence battery.

Gibraltar has the Royal Gibraltar Regiment, part of the Queen's Division. This has two Regular infantry companies and one Reserve company. There is an artillery troop (105mm light guns) in the HQ Company.

Around 100 military personnel, along with some 1,300 civilian personnel, are in Iraq to help train their forces and support operations against ISIL (Operation Shader). There had been around 300–400 at one time. Around 800 were in Afghanistan until August 2021 as part of the Kabul Security Force and training mission (Operation Toral). Toral began after Operation Herrick – combat operations – ended in October 2014.

Overall, some 1,300 personnel were deployed in short term training teams in 55 countries according to 2017 figures.

Soldiers from the 3rd Battalion the Parachute Regiment make use of some natural cover in an overwise open area on a Combined Arms Live Fire Exercise in Kenya during Ex Askari Storm in 2020. Throughout the exercise the 16 Air Assault Brigade units also integrated with the Kenyan Defence Force to conduct joint missions, to help bring UK allied integration with Kenya. (45166124.jpg)

9
TRAINING ESTABLISHMENT

Training is under the control of Home Command, with responsibility belonging to Recruiting and Initial Training Command and the Sandhurst Group.

Officer Training

All officers are commissioned through the Royal Military Academy, Sandhurst (44 Supply Squadron RLC is based at Sandhurst, along with the Gurkha Sittang Company). Regular officers complete the 48-week Commissioning Course. These courses begin in January, May and September each year. There are two routes to a Reserve commission. One is through the University Officer Training Corps (UOTC), the second is to begin training through a local Reserve unit. In either case, the individual will then attend Sandhurst to complete training and receive a commission. Courses for Reserve officers begin in July and September and are shorter than for the Regulars.

There are two other routes to a commission. The Professionally Qualified Officer (PQO) course is for those with professional qualifications (e.g., doctors, lawyers, dentists, nurses, chaplains) and lasts 10 weeks. The Late Entry Officers Course is for someone given a commission after a number of years of prior service as a senior NCO or warrant officer. This lasts four weeks for Regulars and two weeks for Reservists.

Soldier Initial (Phase 1) Training

Initial training for new recruits is handled at different sites depending upon the intended arm or service.

Infantry Training Centre Catterick: all Phase 1 training for the infantry. It is also responsible for the Infantry Battle School (Brecon) and Specialist Weapons School (Warminster). ITC Catterick Support Battalion supports the two training battalions and includes 400 Troop RLC. Training for the Foot Guards and Parachute Regiment is two weeks longer than other infantry training.

1st Infantry Training Battalion now has four companies, down from five. 2nd Infantry Training Battalion also caters to specialised infantry training. At one time, and possibly still, it handled Phase 1 training for new infantry recruits and Phase 2 training for Junior Entry Infantry Recruits from AFC Harrogate and Phase 2 training for infantry of the Army Reserve. See below for Infantry Phase 2/3 training at this site.

Officer Cadets march past the front of the Royal Military Academy Sandhurst (RMAS) Old College, followed by instructors and the College Adjutant on horseback, in 2013. (45157190.jpg)

Army Training Centre Pirbright

1st Army Training Regiment Pirbright
- Jackson Company [Adjutant General's Corps]
- Chevasse Company [Royal Army Medical Corps]
- 59 (Asten) Battery RA

2nd Army Training Regiment Pirbright
- 1 (Fowler) Squadron Royal Corps of Signals
- 108 (The Princess Royal's) Squadron RLC
- 28 Squadron RE
- Caen Squadron RAC
- D Company

ATC Pirbright delivers Phase 1 training for Army Air Corps, Army Medical Services, REME, Corps of Army Music, RAC, Royal Artillery, Royal Signals, RLC, Adjutant General's Corps, and Intelligence Corps. It is usually obvious from designations which units handle which corps, although unclear who handles the REME and AAC. D Company, 2nd ATR Pirbright is responsible for Phase 1 training for recruits joining the Army Reserve, mainly serving the 7th and 11th Brigades and London District.

Army Training Regiment Winchester

ATR Winchester handles Phase 1 training for Standard Entry recruits in the RAC, AAC, Royal Artillery, Royal Engineers, Royal Signals, RLC, REME, Adjutant General's Corps, Royal Army Medical Corps, and Intelligence Corps. The site was due to close down in 2021, later extended to 2024 and then 2026.

Army Training Regiment Grantham

Primary location for Phase 1 training for recruits joining the Army Reserve. There are some other Army Training Units for the Reserve in various parts of the country: North East (Strensall), Northern Ireland (Ballykinler), North West (Alcatar), Scotland (Redford Barracks), South (Pirbright), Wales (Cardiff), West Midlands (Telford), and Wessex (Exeter). The site was due to close in 2020, later extended to 2024 and then 2028.

Army Foundation College Harrogate

Trains 16- and 17-year-olds to become Junior Soldiers in the various regiments and corps of the Army. The 49-week (long) course is for those joining the infantry, Royal Armoured Corps/Household Cavalry, Royal Artillery and some Royal Logistic Corps roles. The 23-week (short) course is for those joining courses with longer Phase 2 training: Royal Electrical and Mechanical Engineers, Royal Engineers, Royal Signals, Adjutant General's Corps, Royal Army Medical Corps, Army Air Corps and some Royal Logistic Corps roles.

Trade (Phase 2/3) Training

Armour Centre [Bovington]

The AFV Training Group has three schools delivering training in the three disciplines of armour: communications, driving and

A photograph from 2014 showing some 400 junior soldiers passing out from the Army Foundation College at Harrogate. (York-2014-006-AFCHarrogatePassOff-246.jpg)

maintenance, and gunnery. Gunnery training is conducted at Lulworth, the other courses at Bovington. These are handled by the AFV Schools Regiment. There is also an RAC Training Regiment, which is the holding unit for new personnel as they attend training. All except for those joining the Household Cavalry (who would already have been approved by them) must select a regiment (providing several, in order of preference); they will then have their training made specific to the regiment to which assigned.

Infantry Training Centre [Catterick]

The Combat Infantryman's Course is combined Phase 1/2 training for recruits. Pegasus Company (P Company) handles all pre-parachute selection courses for Regular and Reserve personnel. The Basic Parachute Course itself is conducted at RAF Brize Norton. The Army School of Ceremonial [sic] covers musical skills (the Drumming Wing) and courses covering drill for NCOs (The All Arms Drill Wing). There is also a school of bagpipe music and highland drumming.

There is also an Infantry Battle School at Brecon, which runs command and leadership training, infantry tactics training, and weapons training. It is attended by officers and soldiers.

The Support Weapons School, Warminster, trains infantrymen as well as soldiers from other arms and services, Royal Marines, and Royal Air Force Regiment. It has three divisions: mortar, fire support, communications and information systems.

The Gurkha Mandalay Company serves in the OPFOR role at the Infantry Battle School.

The Challenegr 2 MBT known as Megatron is seen here on a road system at the the Armoured Trials and Development Unit (ATDU) in Bovington in 2016. (45161517.jpg)

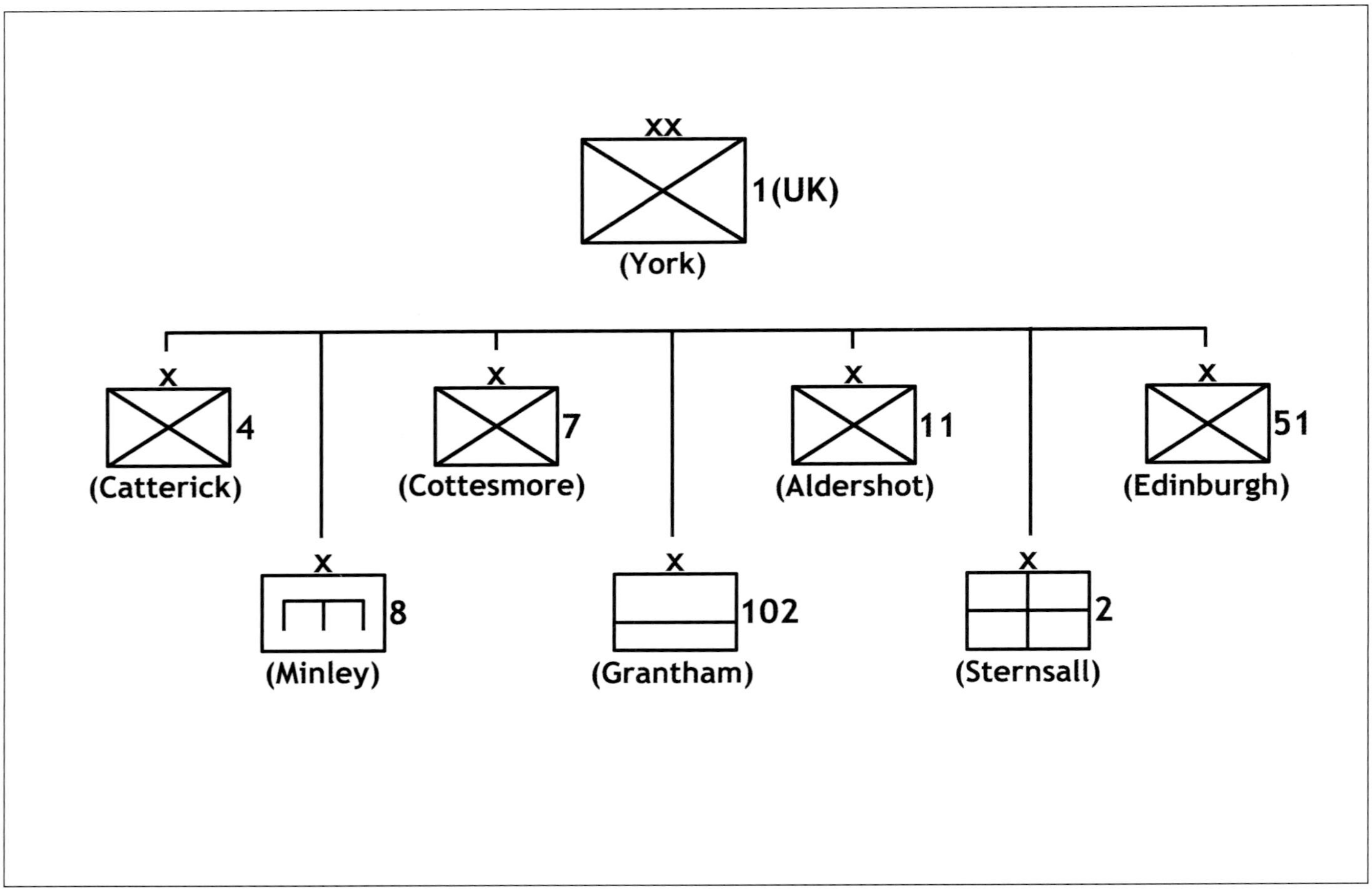

This photograph from 2011 shows an aerial view of the then-new Single Living Accommodation (SLA) blocks built under Project SLAM at Richmondshire Lines, Catterick Garrison, North Yorkshire. (45152852.jpg)

Royal School of Artillery [Larkhill]

14th Regiment RA

1st Battery RA 'The Blazers' [supports all in camp and non-firing training]

24th (Irish) Battery RA [Phase 2 training for all new artillery personnel]

34th (Seringapatam) Battery RA [Phase 3 training: young officer and gunnery career courses, artillery command systems and strike and targeting]

Royal School of Military Engineering [Chatham]

The Royal School of Military Engineering (RSME) Group handles not only training in all of the engineering disciplines, but also military working dogs and their handlers, EOD and ammunition technicians, and search operators.

- 1 RSME Regiment provides artisan engineer training; some trades training can last 53 weeks. It has an RHQ and the 24 and 36 Training Squadrons RE.
- The Professional Engineering Wing provides training to RE professional engineers and technicians (Chartered Engineer and Incorporated Engineer).
- 3 RSME Regiment at Minley is the initial stop for all sappers after Phase 1 training. Skills taught include demolitions, bridging, watermanship, water supply, force protection, basic field engineering and mine warfare. The regiment also has a management and leadership course for all newly-selected lance corporals and corporals. The regiment has an RHQ, the 55 and 57 Training Squadrons RE, and the 63 Training Support Squadron RE.
- The Royal Engineers Warfare Wing trains all RE communications specialists, along with infantry assault pioneers. They also have command, leadership and management courses for all senior NCOs, warrant officers and officers. Officers just commissioned from Sandhurst go through a 27-week engineering course.
- The Defence Animal Training Regiment is at Melton Mowbray, Leicestershire. It has three squadrons: Canine Training, Equine Training, and Veterinary Training.
- Defence Explosive Ordnance Disposal, Munitions and Search Training Regiment at Bicester and Kineton has four specialist squadrons: munitions, search, conventional munitions disposal, and IED disposal. They also provide training to civil police on EOD and Search. The official opening was 13 March 2013, although training began September 2012. The regiment can run 4,000 students through 200 courses a year; there are 73 different courses in all.
- The Defence Counter Chemical Biological Radiological and Nuclear Centre (DCBRNC) I at Winterbourne Gunner, Wiltshire.

The Royal Military School of Music at Twickenham has been subordinated to this group. They handle all musical training for the Army. In September 2021, initial trade training for Army [Royal School of Military Engineering] musicians moved to the new Alford Schools of Military Music at Portsmouth, alongside the Royal Marines Band trainees. Training will remain within each service.

Royal School of Signals [Blandford]

11th (Royal School of Signals) Signal Regiment: conducts all Phase 2 and 3 training for new Signals personnel, as well as later specialised training. The school is part of the Defence School of Communications and Information Systems.

1 (Fowler) Squadron forms part of 2 Army Training Regiment
2 (Catterick) Squadron
3 (Harrogate) Squadron
4 (Military Training) Squadron
5 (Maresfield) Squadron

Army Aviation Centre [Middle Wallop]

2 (Training) Regiment AAC
676 Squadron AAC [admin support for Phase 2 training for groundcrew]
668 (Training) Squadron AAC [delivers Phase 3 training for groundcrew; also includes junior and senior command courses and the ground support commander course for officers]
7 (Training) Regiment AAC
671 Squadron AAC [Lynx, Gazelle, Bell 212 conversion to type training]
673 Squadron AAC [Apache conversion to type training]

Defence Helicopter Flying School [RAF Shawbury]

Rebadged in 2020 as No 1 Flying Training School. The school trains all helicopter pilots for all three services.

2 Maritime Wing
660 Squadron AAC [basic rotary wing training]
705 Naval Air Squadron AAC [basic rotary wing training]
No 202 Squadron RAF [maritime and mountain flying training]

9 Regiment AAC
670 Squadron AAC [advanced rotary wing training; Airbus H135 and Juno HT1]
No 60 Squadron RAF [advanced rotary wing training; Airbus H135 and Juno HT1]

The Defence School of Electronic and Mechanical Engineering [Lyneham]

8 Training Battalion REME conducts training for Army and RAF personnel, with up to 1,500 personnel under its control. This was formed in 2015 from two existing battalions (10 Training Battalion REME at Borden conducted training for vehicle mechanics, armourers, recovery mechanics, metalsmiths and technical support specialists and also conducts equipment courses; 11 Training Battalion REME at Arborfield conducted training for aircraft technicians, avionics technicians and electronics technicians). In addition to driving training, the courses are: recovery mechanic training, armourer training, metalsmith training, vehicle mechanic training, technical support specialist training, and technician (aircraft/avionics/electronics) training. Courses range from seven to 65 weeks. 8 Training Battalion REME is paired with the RAF's No. 4 School of Technical Training at MOD St Athan. This is one of four schools within the Defence College of Technical Training.

Defence School of Transport [Normandy Barracks, Leconfield]

This was formed in 1977 as an Army school to consolidate several military driver training establishments. Since 1996 it provides driver and transport management training for the Army, RAF, and Royal Marines and was given its present name. 110 Training Squadron RLC handles RLC personnel as they go from Phase 1 to their chosen trade. After obtaining their license they go to their units for Phase 3 training. The Military Support Squadron performs the same Phase 2 role for personnel from other cap badges. The Driver Training Squadron provides training on a variety of higher license types. The Specialist Training Squadron provides specialist operator or instructor courses on any number of specialist vehicles. The MT [Mechanical Transport] Management Squadron provides courses from junior to senior MT management. The [Defence School of Transport] Communication Information Systems Squadron provides basic and advanced courses for regimental and reserve signallers (i.e., in units other than the Royal Corps of Signals).

Officer Commissions

Direct enlistment officers leave Sandhurst as 2nd Lieutenants with a Short Service Commission (SSC). This is for a minimum of three years; six in the Army Air Corps, given the length and expense of flying training. The commission can be extended for up to eight years, after which these officers leave the Army without a pension. The SSC is basically for those who do not want to commit to a long career but wish to benefit from Army training and experience.

After two years on an SSC, if recommended, an officer can apply for an Intermediate Regular Commission (IRC). These officers leave the Army after 18 years of service and after age 40. They are entitled to a lump sum and monthly payments, which convert at age 65 to a further lump sum and a pension.

After two years on an IRC, if recommended, an officer can apply for a Regular Commission. This offers a full career of 35 years or until age 60, whichever occurs first. They receive a lump sum and an immediate pension from age 55.

Senior NCOs and warrant officers can qualify for a late entry commission. They attend a special late officer entry course at Sandhurst.

Professionally qualified officers can be commissioned if they are doctors, dentists, nurses, lawyers, pharmacists, physiotherapists, veterinary surgeons, environmental health officers, operating department practitioners and chaplains with the relevant degrees and experience. Those who commit to the Army while still in professional school can receive support payments ('bursary') and a lump sum (the 'golden handshake') upon commissioning. They begin at a higher rank than direct enlistment officers. A doctor without experience, for example, would normally start as a captain. The minimum commitment is four years if the Army helped pay for their schooling.

Perhaps unique to the British Army is the Army Officer Internship, formerly known as the gap year commission or, more formally, the Short Service (Limited) Commission. Following a shortened training period at Sandhurst, these officers serve six to 18 months (before, during or after university), generally shadowing platoon or troop commanders; they cannot deploy on operations. They can then leave without further obligation (which most do) or apply for a Regular or Army Reserve commission.

The H135 Juno (Juno HT Mk.1) provides the basic rotary wing training role with No.1 Flying Training School (1 FTS) at RAF Shawbury, the oldest military pilot training school in the world. With all but a handful of the UK's frontline military helicopters equipped with glass cockpits, the H135 (Juno HT1) has brought helicopter training into the modern era. It also ensures continuity and a logical progression for Royal Air Force, Royal Navy and Army Air Corps students through the UK Military Flying Training System. The type serves with 60 Squadron at RAF Shawbury, and 202 Squadron at RAF Valley which delivers maritime, mountain, and search and rescue training to helicopter aircrew. (shy-20230117-12-2.jpg)

A Mastiff 2 armoured vehicle leads the way at the Leconfield testing track in North Yorkshire. Mastiff is a heavily armoured, 6 x six-wheel-drive patrol vehicle which carries eight people, plus two crew. (45153080.jpg)

10
BRITISH ARMY RANKS

Other Ranks

Table 3: Other Ranks and Insignia

Rank [NATO code]	Insignia
Private [OR-1 and OR-2] Private [OR-1 and OR-2]	no insignia
Lance Corporal [OR-3]	single bar chevron
Corporal [OR-4]	two-bar chevron
Sergeant [OR-5 and OR-6]	three-bar chevron
Staff Sergeant/Colour Sergeant [OR-7]	three-bar chevron with crown above
Warrant Officer class 2 [OR-8]	plain crown (CSM), crown within a laurel wreath
Warrant Officer class 1 [OR-9]	the Royal Arms; the Royal Arms within a laurel wreath for Corps RSMs and other senior WO1s

A number of regiments and corps have alternative titles in lieu of private; e.g., Trooper in the cavalry and SAS; Airtrooper in the Army Air Corps, Guardsman in the Foot Guards; Fusilier in fusilier regiments; Gunner in the RA; Sapper in the RE; Signaller in the Royal Signals; Craftsman in the REME; Rifleman in The Rifles and the Royal Gurkha Rifles; Ranger in The Royal Irish Regiment and the Ranger Regiment; and Kingsman in the Duke of Lancaster's Regiment.

In the Royal Artillery, a lance corporal is a lance bombardier and a corporal is a bombardier.

The Rifles use the old spelling of Serjeant. This was apparently in common use in the Army into the 1930s.

The Household Cavalry have different titles and insignia for these ranks, completely avoiding the word 'Sergeant'. For example, their Sergeant equivalent is called a Corporal of Horse and a corporal is a Lance Corporal of Horse; a Staff Sergeant is a Staff Corporal. Their insignia of rank are also different.

Officers

Table 4: Commissioned Ranks and Insignia

Rank [NATO code]	Insignia
Second Lieutenant [OF-1]	one star
Lieutenant [OF-1]	two stars
Captain [OF-2]	three stars
Major [OF-3]	crown
Lieutenant Colonel [OF-4]	crown above one star
Colonel [OF-5]	crown above two stars
Brigadier [OF-6]	crown above three stars (lower two side by side)
Major General [OF-7]	crossed sword and baton, star above
Lieutenant General [OF-8]	crossed sword and baton, crown above
General [OF-9]	crossed sword and baton, with crown over star above
Field Marshal [OF-10]	crossed batons on a laurel wreath, with crown above

The standard star is based on the Bath Star but certain regiments wear the Eversley Star. The Household Division wear versions of the Garter, Thistle or St. Patrick's Star. The standard crown is the St. Edward's Crown, although field officers of the Household Division wear the Imperial Crown.

In the British Army, majors normally serve as company/battery/troop commanders, unlike most other armies where that is a captain's command. Brigadier is a field officer rank rather than a general officer rank.

Field Marshal is now an honorary or ceremonial rank. Peter Inge, now Baron Inge, received the last promotion of a serving officer in 1994, upon assuming the position as Chief of the Defence Staff. After him, individuals appointed as Chief of the Defence Staff were no longer promoted to Field Marshal or the equivalent (Marshal of the Royal Air Force or Admiral of the Fleet) upon assuming the post. They are, however, normally given life peerages upon retirement.

The next two promotions after Baron Inge came in 2012. HRH Charles, then Prince of Wales and now King Charles III, and Charles Guthrie, Lord Guthrie of Craigiebank (a former Chief of the Defence Staff, retiring in 2001). The most recent was Michael Walker, Baron Walker of Aldringham in 2014 (also a former Chief of the Defence Staff, retiring in 2006.[7]

SOURCES

Dr. Graham Watson, a longtime friend and colleague, has spent a lifetime acquiring information on the British Army, and has been a regular source of details not found elsewhere during the years I was working on this project. He and Cliff Lord were selected by the Royal Signals to write their most recent official history: *The Royal Corps of Signals: Unit Histories of the Corps (1920-2001) and its Antecedents* (Solihull, West Midlands: Helion and Company Limited, 2003). We collaborated well over a decade ago on *The British Army in Germany (BAOR and After): An Organizational History 1947-2004* (Tiger Lily Publications LLC for Orbat.com, 2005) and more recently on *The Corps of Royal Engineers: Organization and Units 1889-2018* (Tiger Lily Books, 2018).

Useful as a background reference is James Tanner, *The British Army since 2000* (Elite 202) (Oxford: Osprey Publishing Ltd, 2014). This includes the initial changes under *Army 2020* as well as information on uniforms, weapons, and equipment. As with many other Osprey publications, it is well illustrated. Another useful background source is the last of Charles Heyman's once on-going series, *The British Army Guide 2016-2017* (Barnsley: Pen & Sword Books Ltd, n.d.). This also covers the beginnings of *Army 2020* and, like its predecessors, is a fairly comprehensive look at the Army in particular and the defence establishment overall.

The British Army's web site (www.army.mod.uk/) can be a frustrating resource. Based on years of viewing, it appears that updates are left to the particular formation or unit. This led to quite different levels of detail and updates were not always on a timely basis. It could be difficult at times to determine the date of updates or what year is being referred to for an operation or training deployment. In addition, other kinds of material (such as documents relating to *Army 2020*, *Army 2020 Refine*, and so forth) can come or go and you always need to download anything you find as soon as you see it. Even where something does not just disappear, URLs are subject to change as they redesign different parts of the site. There is less information available than formerly, such as elimination of brief unit histories once found there. However, the corps and regiment pages all now have a standard format, even though the amount of detail can still vary. What is there is official, but do not count on it necessarily being complete or current. However, it does seem to be getting much better at keeping up to date. The News section in particular can be a useful guide to changes and activities. On 1 October 2024 the British Army completely redesigned their web site, heading it 'The Army The Nation Needs: Protecting the United Kingdom and helping it prosper by fighting and winning our battles from the land.' 'The Army the Nation Needs' was the theme of Army Expo 2024 held the prior month. They believe that this revised site will provide easier journeys to find the topics you are interested in, along with interactive features and refreshed and updated content. For those long used to the former design, this may take some getting used to the first few visits. All references to the British Army website refer to the version prior to the 1 October 2024 redesign.

A useful even if now dated document is *The Location and Work Force Requirements of British Army Units, by Corps (as at 1 November 2018)*. This includes the actual strength of each unit, under a column headed 'Current Liability.' This was prepared in response to a question raised in Parliament: questions-statements.parliament.uk/written-questions/detail/2018-11-22/194616

CGS's Message to the Army Implementing the Future Army Structure, 16 December 2004. URL no longer available. See also his earlier Delivering Security in a Changing World, Future Capabilities, at www.mod.uk/issues/security/cm6269/cgs.htm.

Securing Britain in an Age of Uncertainty: The Strategic Defence and Security Review. (Cm 7948, October 2010). assets.publishing.service.gov.uk/government/uploads/system/uploads/attachment_data/file/62482/strategic-defence-security-review.pdf

Transforming the British Army: Modernising to face an unpredictable future. (July 2012). issuu.com/openbriefing/docs/britisharmy2020

Transforming the British Army: An Update—July 2013 cdn0.scrvt.com/8a7fb8c945e2d564ea89e3facb7da507/df57f9b3ba635dfa/448ac4adb5b8/Army2020_Report_v2.pdf

Combat Capability for the Future (British Army, November 2013). URL unavailable

RAND Corporation. *Setting Priorities in the Age of Austerity: British, French and German Experiences*. Prepared for the United States Army. Published 2013 by the RAND Corporation; written by Michael Shurkin.

Future Reserves 2020. The Independent Commission to Review the United Kingdom's Reserve Forces. (London: July 2011). assets.publishing.service.gov.uk/government/uploads/system/uploads/attachment_data/file/35891/20121123_consultation_fr20.pdf

McBride, Lorraine, 'Basing: On Track, On Time and On Budget', *Defence Focus* (Issue # 269, April 2013), pp. 14ff.

National Security Strategy and Strategic Defence and Security Review 2015: A Secure and Prosperous United Kingdom (Cm 9161, November 2015), www.gov.uk/government/publications/national-security-strategy-and-strategic-defence-and-security-review-2015

The plans for the British military in between *Army 2020 Refine* and *Future Soldier* are contained in *Defence in a Competitive Age* (Secretary of State for Defence, 30 March 2021), www.gov.uk/government/publications/defence-in-a-competitive-age/defence-in-a-competitive-age-accessible-version. This is an online document, not a pdf that can be downloaded.

Planned moves for November 2020 are contained in *In Front: British Army Newsletter*, Summer 2020, Issue 5, www.army.mod.uk/media/10192/adr009405_in_front_5.pdf.

Modernising the Army's armoured fighting vehicles, House of Commons Briefing Paper No 08186, 26 April 2018, researchbriefings.files.parliament.uk/documents/CBP-8186/CBP-8186.pdf. is a very good discussion of the time and efforts (usually in vain) to update or replace various vehicles and a look at the (now abandoned) strike brigades. From the Summary section at the beginning: 'The Army does not have a good track record when it comes to acquiring armoured vehicles from the core budget. The last thirty years is awash with cancelled, suspended or modified programmes....' As discussed in this work, it appears that Ajax may well be added to the list of failures. Strikingly, the Army opted out of the multi-nation Boxer family of vehicles, and only recently changed course and decided to acquire them, having lost more than a decade in the interim.

The Defence Equipment Plan 2021-2031. (Ministry of Defence 2022). assets.publishing.service.gov.uk/media/620fc427d3bf7f4f0981a158/Defence_Equipment_Plan_2021.pdf

Future Soldier Guide, www.army.mod.uk/media/15057/adr010310-futuresoldierguide_30nov.pdf

Integrated Review Refresh 2023: Responding to a more contested and volatile world. (March 2023, CPB 811. Presented to Parliament by the Prime Minister by Command of His Majesty.) assets.publishing.service.gov.uk/government/uploads/system/uploads/attachment_data/file/1142616/11857435_NS_IR_Refresh_2023_Supply_AllPages_Revision_4_WEB_PDF_NoCrops_-_gov.uk.pdf

Ministry of Defence, *Defence's response to a more contested and volatile world* (Presented to Parliament by the Secretary of State for Defence by Command of His Majesty 18th July 2023), assets.publishing.service.gov.uk/government/uploads/system/uploads/attachment_data/file/1171269/Defence_Command_Paper_2023_Defence_s_response_to_a_more_contested_and_volatile_world.pdf

The most useful site for the Gurkhas is The Gurkha Brigade Association, www.gurkhabde.com/. This has a section on history, as well as a complete list of current Gurkha units in the British Army.

The British government does not publish anything on their special forces. My major resource here was Elite UK Forces, www.eliteukforces.info/.

Information on RAF and RN helicopter squadrons and aircraft are from the RAF website, www.raf.mod.uk/ and RN website, www.royalnavy.mod.uk/. The Royal Marines are embedded within the RN web site, and that was the main source for details on their ground units. The RAF Regiment is found within the RAF web site.

Colin Mackie's "Army Commands 1860-" is an amazing compendium of Army organisation and formations and officers, often including chiefs of staff and other appointments. The most recent version was updated as of July 2022. It is available for download from his web site, gulabin.com. From the Home Page, click on British Armed Forces (1860-). He has documents on the Army, Royal Navy, Royal Air Force, and Ministry of Defence and Tri-Service senior appointments.

Jack Watling and Justin Bronk discuss the strike brigade concept in *Strike: From Concept to Force* (RUSI Occasional Paper, June 2019), with their suggestions for improvement. A more critical look, inspired by their paper, is provided by Gabriele Molinelli, *RUSI tries to fix STRIKE, but can it be fixed?*, also on ukarmedforcescommentary.blogspot.com. (His paper contains a link to the Watling and Bronk piece.) This is also discussed by Lieutenant Colonel Martin A. Smith, 'The STRIKE Brigade: the Army's Battlecruiser for the 21st Century?', pp. 32–37 and William F. Owen, 'Be Different to Be Better', pp. 38–45; both in *British Army Review*, Number 178 (Summer 2020). A critical reaction to their introduction is provided by Stuart Crawford, 'Strike Brigades: Back to the Future?', ukdj July 8, 2019, ukdefencejournal.org.uk/strike-brigades-back-to-the-future/. Whether or not the strike brigade was a good idea, it is being abandoned before implementation, although the articles remain interesting and may yet become relevant again. With replacement of the Warrior by the Boxer down the road, the armoured brigade combat teams will become not unlike the strike brigades, simply substituting an armoured regiment for one of the Ajax-equipped armoured cavalry regiments.

There are innumerable Wikipedia pages on the British Army and its formations and units. Prepared by different individuals at different times, they are not always consistent with each other. However, used carefully, they often provide information which cannot be found anywhere else. Importantly, they often have links to useful online documents and sources, such as answers to freedom of information requests or Parliamentary Inquiries, or even unit Twitter and Instagram announcements. However, links back to the British Army web page are often unproductive, either resulting in pages which no longer have the information or 'page cannot be found' results.

An interesting collection of essays considering all aspects of recent British military policy and the various services is contained in King's College London, Centre for Defence Studies, *The Integrated Review in Context: Defence and Security in Focus* (October 2021), at www.kcl.ac.uk/warstudies/assets/ir-in-context-defence-and-security-in-focus.pdf. This is actually their second volume of collected essays on the Integrated Review. The fall of Afghanistan and the AUKUS agreement (increased defence cooperation by the US, UK and Australia) occurred after the first volume appeared. The first volume was published in July 2021 as *The Integrated Review in Context: A Strategy Fit for the 2020s?*, at www.kcl.ac.uk/warstudies/assets/the-integrated-review-in-context.pdf. It is, however, more oriented towards political issues with much less emphasis or information on the services.

Following are other reports, documents, or other material referred to in the text or relied on. These are listed in the approximate order in which they are referred to in the text:

'The Army's Firm Base', *The British Army Journal*, 2011, at army.newsdeskmedia.com/british-army-2011/the-armys-firm-base

Ministry of Defence, Quarterly service personnel statistics 1 January 2024, www.gov.uk/government/statistics/quarterly-service-personnel-statistics-2024/quarterly-service-personnel-statistics-1-january-2024#uk-service-personnel

Some earlier versions were consulted in earlier stages of research.

Ministry of Defence, 'UK armed forces equipment and formations', 9 September 2021 and 11 October 2022 versions, at (1) www.gov.uk/government/collections/uk-armed-forces-equipment-and-formations and (2) www.gov.uk/government/statistics/uk-armed-forces-equipment-and-formations-2022/uk-armed-forces-equipment-and-formations-2022. These are both very detailed documents.

The next published version, 'UK armed forces equipment and formations 2023' (updated 8 March 2024), www.gov.uk/government/statistics/uk-armed-forces-equipment-and-formations-2023/uk-armed-forces-equipment-and-formations-2023 is a very summary document. As indicated in the text, it has very little information on almost all individual vehicles and equipment.

The Economist. 'Master and commander,' The Economist, October 16th-22nd, 2021, p. 50

'Mean Streets', 444 The Economist 9309 (August 20th–26th 2022), p. 51

'Don't stop spending', 447 The Economist 9346 (13 May 2023), p. 42

'Losing muscle', 450 The Economist 9382 (February 3rd–9th, 2024), pp. 46–47

'New UK Army chief issues Russia rallying cry', BBC News 19 June 2022, www.bbc.com/news/uk-6185', 8476.

Anglim, Dr Simon, 'Global Britain, Global Army? The Review and Land Warfare', in King's College London, Centre for Defence Studies, *The Integrated Review in Context: Defence and Security in Focus* (October 2021), at www.kcl.ac.uk/warstudies/assets/ir-in-context-defence-and-security-in- focus.pdf.

Operation Cerberus. www.army.mod.uk/news-and-events/news/2022/10/exercise-cerberus-22-british-armys-largest-european-exercise-in-a-decade/.

'Army chief sets out plan for next generation of war fighters' (12 September 2023), www.army.mod.uk/news-and-events/news/2023/09/army-chief-sets-out-plan-for-next-generation-of-war-fighters/

Royal Irish in light recce role. The British Army's Global Response Force (GRF) is being put through its paces with demanding training on Salisbury Plain Training Area, www.army.mod.uk/news-and-events/news/2023/05/global-response-force-tested-on-iconic-salisbury-plain/

Gordon, Gavin. 'Royal Marines to form new commando force in armed forces shake-up', *Evening Standard*, 22 March 2021, www.standard.co.uk/news/uk/royal-marines-ben-wallace-army-defence-ministry-of-defence-b925440.html

'Watch: What is the Future Commando Force? (23 March 2021), www.forces.net/news/royal-marines/what-royal-marines-future-commando-force

'Defence Command Paper: What It Means For Each Service,' www.forces.net/news/defence-command-paper-what-it-means-each-service

'Inside Camp Viking – the new Arctic operations base for UK commandos', You Tube, www.youtube.com/watch?v=dpEiSk2ZgFM

'Special Operations: British Rangers Return,' StrategyPage.com (10 May 2021),

www.strategypage.com/htmw/htsf/articles/20210510.aspx.

'New Army Ranger Regiment: What We Know So Far', Forces.net, (6 April 2021), www.forces.net/news/new-army-ranger-regiment-what-we-know-so-far.

'Introducing the New RAF Police Operating Model' (12 February 2021), at www.raf.mod.uk/our-organisation/force-protection/news/introducing-the-new-raf-police-operating-model/

'The Next Generation of RAF Police,' WO Simon (Jimmy) Brown, RAF Police Association, rafpassociation.com/general-rafpa-news/the-next-generation-of-raf-police-by-wo-simon-jimmy-brown-pmwo/

'The British Army could have an AJAX squadron this summer,' 4 March 2021, www.army-technology.com/news/the-british-army-could-have-an-ajax-squadron-this-summer/

Watling, Dr Jack, 'The British Army's Greek Tragedy,' *RUSI*, 22 July 2021. rusi.org/explore-our-research/publications/commentary/british-armys-greek-tragedy

Beale, Jonathan, BBC News, 3 June 2021, 'Major design flaws in Army's new armoured vehicles, report shows.' www.bbc.com/news/uk-57348573.

Minister for Defence Procurement September 2021 statement on Ajax, questions-statements.parliament.uk/written-statements/detail/2021-09-06/hcws260

Neville, Leigh, *The British Army in Afghanistan 2006-14: Task Force Helmand* (Osprey Elite 205) (Oxford: Osprey Publishing Ltd, 2015). [On the introduction of protected patrol vehicles]

On the Archer acquisition, www.army.mod.uk/news-and-events/news/2023/10/british-army-s-first-archer-gun-has-arrived-on-uk-soil/

'Watchkeeper Armed' StrategyPage.com (28 October 2015); www.strategypage.com/htmw/htairfo/articles/20151028.aspx.

'British Army flying new elite attack helicopters', www.gov.uk/government/news/british-army-flying-new-elite-attack-helicopters

Army Dress Regulations (All Ranks) (Ministry of Defence, January 2011), assets.publishing.service.gov.uk/government/uploads/system/uploads/attachment_data/file/626107/2017-03109.pdf

The Rifles Dress Guidance, Summer 2015, web.archive.org/web/20151203224525/http://storage.the-rifles.co.uk/downloads/Rifles_Dress_Guidance.pdf

'His Majesty The King's Coronation heralds new era for British Army cap badges', www.army.mod.uk/news-and-events/news/2023/03/his-majesty-the-kings-coronation-heralds-new-era-for-british-army-cap-badges/. This contains illustrations of all of the Army's cap badges.

NOTES

Chapter 2

1 RAND was originally created by the US Air Force and became an organisation devoted to improving policy through research and analysis, often for US military customers. This particular report was requested by the US Army.

Chapter 3

1 Serving Regular Reserves are ex Regulars with a statutory liability for service; only those serving under a fixed-term contract on active service are now counted.

2 Trained professionals who carry out certain support or specialist tasks while also maintaining a civilian career.

Chapter 4

1 The Royal Fleet Auxiliary (RFA) is a uniformed civilian branch of the RN, manning ships that provide logistical support to the RN and RM.

Chapter 7

1 While sometimes shown as II (Parachute) Squadron, the squadron's web page indicates that it was an airborne assault squadron from 1962 to 1992, at which point it resumed its role as a light squadron.

2 3 Tactical Police Sqn is mentioned in the entry for the Specialist Police Wing, but not in the list of squadrons, where the only RAF Police '3' is a reserve squadron.

Chapter 10

1 Walker's promotion was part of the 2014 Queen's birthday honours, along with similar promotions for Admiral the Lord Boyce and Air Chief Marshal the Lord Stirrup, also former Chiefs of the Defence Staff. This was termed a promotion to 'honorary 5-star rank' and followed by the comment, 'The appointment to honorary 5-star rank is a promotion that can be given by the sovereign alone and is made sparingly.' Guthrie's promotion in 2012 to 'the honorary rank of field marshal' was made in the same announcement as Prince Charles' promotion to the highest ranks in all three services.

ABOUT THE AUTHOR

Richard A. Rinaldi is a graduate of Swarthmore College and Yale University. Formerly a human resources specialist with the federal government, he has a long-term interest in military history. His *The United States Army in World War I: Ground Units, 1917—1919* was published in 2005; *Order of Battle of the British Army 1914* in 2008; and *British Armour and Recce in the Second World War: Units, Organization and Equipment* in 2013. He cooperated with Ravi Rikhye on *Indian Army Order of Battle* in 2011. He has also teamed with Dr Graham Watson on *The British Army in Germany (BAOR and After): An Organizational History 1947-2004* published in 2005 and *The Corps of Royal Engineers: Organization and Units, 1889-2018* in 2018.